A Taste for Health

Delicious Low-Fat Low-Cholesterol Recipes

Contents

Your Health	3
Definitions	4
Watch Out for Salt	5
Cooking Tips	6-8
Appetizers	9-19
Soups	20-22
Salads & Dressings	23-25
Meat	26-34
Poultry	35-41
Fish	42-47
Pasta & Grains	48-50
Vegetables	51-56
Breads	57-70
Desserts	71-83
Index	84-88

Dedication and Foreword

This cookbook is dedicated to the participants in the Coronary Primary Prevention Trial of 1973-1984. This was the first clinical testing in the United States and Canada to study whether lowering serum cholesterol will reduce deaths caused by cardiovascular disease.

Participants in the study were between the ages of 35 and 59. All were men because of the high incidence of heart attacks in males in this age range in American society.

Twelve centers were chosen to participate in the study so that different regions of the United States and Canada would be represented. Some recipes in this cookbook are suggestive of these regional differences.

This is a prudent diet, not a radical one, and is designed to lower blood cholesterol levels. The recipes are moderately low in cholesterol and fat.

The amounts per serving of oil or margarine and meat (including meat, fish and poultry) are listed after each recipe.

The recipes were painstakingly tested at the Iowa Lipid Clinic at The University of Iowa. Fat and cholesterol content was calculated by a professionally trained food scientist, Steve Wonder, and a registered dietitian, Laura Vailas.

There were taste panel evaluations of all recipes. Some were tested three and four times before the recipe was deemed acceptable. When questions arose as to a specific type of product to use, such as a type of cheese, elaborate testing sessions were arranged using several samples of the same product, each with a different ingredient. During all tasting sessions, every effort was made to standardize the taste test. The taste panel members were instructed not to compare results or to discuss results during the tasting session.

A Taste For Health
Delicious Low-Fat Low-Cholesterol Recipes
© Copyright 1984
The University of Iowa

A revised edition of
MODIFIED MAGIC: Recipes from the Coronary Primary Prevention Trial
© Copyright 1982
The University of Iowa

ISBN 0-941016-16-1
Library of Congress catalog #84-80259
Published by Penfield Press, 215 Brown Street, Iowa City, Iowa 52240

Cover photographs © by Joan Liffring-Zug
Graphic design by Esther Feske
Typesetting by Compositors, Inc., Cedar Rapids, Iowa
Printing by Julin Printing Co., Monticello, Iowa

More Cookbooks
More cookbooks are available by mail from Penfield Press. 1984 prices, subject to change.
A Taste for Health. This book, by mail: $5.95, 2 for $10.75, 3 for $14.85, postpaid to one address.
Write for our complete list of publications.
Penfield Press
215 Brown St.
Iowa City, Iowa 52240

Your Health

Many persons are advised by physicians to limit cholesterol and saturated fat intake. One of the most serious handicaps to following a low cholesterol diet is the lack of variety of easy or interesting recipes. As a contribution to those who enjoy eating but wish to modify fat intake, we offer this work of carefully developed recipes.

It is important to understand the premises underlying the recipes in this volume. The Coronary Primary Prevention Trial advocated a control diet which was modestly low in cholesterol content, e.g. 400 milligrams (mg) per day with some reduction in saturated fat and increase in polyunsaturated fat to achieve a P/S (polyunsaturated fat to saturated fat ratio) of 0.6 to 1.0. To achieve this goal, the consumption of amounts and types of meat, dairy products, eggs, margarine and oil was controlled. At the same time, miscellaneous sources of saturated fat such as chocolate candy, coconut or palm oil, and gravy were prohibited. The avoidance of commercially prepared food which might contain animal or hydrogenated vegetable fats is an important challenge for persons on a fat-controlled diet. Skim milk, grain products, fruits and vegetables are permitted in unlimited amount, except where they would contribute to excess energy intake, thus add to body fat.

The recipes in this volume specify the number and size of servings. Moreover, the amounts of meat, dairy products, egg, margarine and oil provided in each serving are indicated below each recipe. If you wish to estimate cholesterol content of a serving, you can use the following conversions: 1 oz. meat, fish or poultry contains approximately 25 mg cholesterol, 1 dairy equivalent has about 30 mg cholesterol, 1 egg contains roughly 250 mg cholesterol, margarine and oil have no cholesterol. Certain seafoods contain little cholesterol, e.g. clams (18 mg/oz.), oysters (13 mg/oz.), tuna (19 mg/oz.), lobster (25 mg/oz.), while shrimp contains 46 mg cholesterol per ounce.

The recipes can be used by anyone who wishes to be prudent in his/her intake of cholesterol and saturated fat. (A note of caution relates to the sodium content of these recipes: some are not particularly low in sodium and would require further modification to fall within the realm of a low sodium diet.) In many cases, old favorites have been modified for the cholesterol-conscious. Other recipes represent innovative alternatives to their high-fat, cholesterol laden counterparts. In all cases, they are delicious and attractive, having been given the stamp of approval by a discriminating panel of judges.

Bon appètit!

Helmut G. Schrott, M.D.
Deputy Director of the
Lipid Research Clinic,
The University of Iowa

Definitions

Lipid is the scientific name for the whole family of naturally occurring fat compounds in the body.

Blood Cholesterol is a lipid made and used in all the body cells. The amount of cholesterol in the blood is a delicate balance depending on several factors: 1) how much our body makes; 2) what we eat; 3) how much our cells use; and 4) how much is broken down and excreted.

Dietary Fat refers to members of the lipid family which are composed of fatty acids and are present in the foods we eat. Two major types of dietary fats, saturated and polyunsaturated, have been shown to affect blood cholesterol levels.

Saturated Fats are in many foods of animal origin, and in some foods from plants. Saturated fats are solid at room temperature. Examples include the fat in meat and dairy products. Examples from plant sources: coconut oil, palm oil and cocoa butter. All saturated fats can increase blood cholesterol levels.

Hydrogenated fats are fats that have been made more saturated by a special chemical process.

Polyunsaturated fats come primarily from plant sources. They are liquid at room temperature. Examples include vegetable oils, salad dressings and fish oil. These fats can decrease blood cholesterol levels.

P/S Ratio is a comparison of polyunsaturated (P) to saturated (S) fat in a diet. It is the amount of polyunsaturated fat in a day's diet divided by the amount of saturated fat in a day's diet.

Atherosclerosis is the process of blood vessel narrowing as a result of fatty deposits on the interior walls of the blood vessels. The disease develops slowly over time, probably beginning in late childhood or early adulthood. Atherosclerosis results in partial or complete blockage of the blood flow by these fatty deposits, leading to cardiovascular disease.

Coronary Heart Disease is caused by atherosclerosis or an accumulation of fatty deposits in the walls of the arteries of the heart. These fatty deposits eventually develop fibrous tissue and the vessel becomes stiffened (or hardened). Decreased blood flow through these damaged vessels can kill heart muscle, resulting in a heart attack.

Watch Out for Salt

Salt helps flavor food, but it is estimated that most people use twice as much as they should. The recipes in this cookbook were designed to be moderately low in cholesterol and fat to reduce blood cholesterol levels. Millions of Americans are also afflicted with high blood pressure, increasing their risk for strokes and heart attacks. Too much salt will aggravate this condition.

To decrease the amount of salt in your diet, use only half as much as ordinary cookbooks call for, and gradually decrease this to as little as possible. Taste all food before salting. Use other flavoring agents, such as herbs, spices, lemon juice and vinegar instead of salt.

Salt is a combination of sodium and chloride. Sodium affects blood pressure. Sodium is found in other flavoring agents such as monosodium glutamate (MSG), soy sauce, chili powder, horseradish, onion flakes and meat tenderizer.

One teaspoon of salt contains 2,300 milligrams of sodium. The American Spice Trade Association provides the following table with the sodium content of spices. Spices in this table may be used as substitutes for the flavoring agents in these recipes.

Sodium Content of Spices

Spice	Milligrams per teaspoon
Allspice	1.4
Basil Leaves	0.4
Bay Leaves	0.3
Caraway Seed	0.4
Cardamon Seed	0.2
Celery Seed	4.1
Cinnamon	0.2
Cloves	4.2
Coriander Seed	0.3
Cumin Seed	2.6
Curry Powder	1.0
Dill Seed	0.2
Fennel Seed	1.9
Garlic Powder	0.1
Ginger	0.5
Mace	1.3
Marjoram	1.3
Mustard Powder	0.1
Nutmeg	0.2
Onion Powder	0.8
Oregano	0.3
Paprika	0.4
Parsley Flakes	5.9
Pepper, Black	0.2
Pepper, Chili	0.2
Pepper, Red	0.2
Pepper, White	0.2
Poppy Seed	0.2
Rosemary Leaves	0.5
Sage	0.1
Savory	0.3
Sesame Seed	0.6
Tarragon	1.0
Thyme	1.2
Turmeric	0.2

Some recipes in this cookbook call for commercial products that are high in sodium, such as dry soup mixes, low-fat processed cheese, canned vegetables, canned soups and dry seasoning mixes. Recipe changes will require testing to taste (a little experimentation on your part). For example, instead of using dry soup mixes, canned vegetables and soups, all of which contribute sodium to the recipes, substitute fresh ingredients.

Cooking Tips

Table of Equivalents

Measure	Equivalent	Fluid Ounces
1 tablespoon	3 teaspoons	0.5
2 tablespoons	⅛ cup	1.0
1 jigger	3 tablespoons	1.5
¼ cup	4 tablespoons	2.0
⅓ cup	5 tablespoons plus 1 teaspoon	2.8
½ cup	8 tablespoons	4.0
1 cup	16 tablespoons	8.0
1 pint	2 cups	16.0
1 quart	4 cups	32.0
1 liter	1 quart plus 3½ tablespoons	33.8
1 gallon	4 quarts	128.0

Weight to Volume Approximations

Rice and Pasta
1 pound of: **uncooked** **cooked**
Rice = 2 cups = 6 cups
Macaroni = 4 cups = 8 cups
Spaghetti = 5 cups = 9 cups

Beans
1 pound of: **uncooked** **cooked**
Kidney = 1⅓ cups = 9 cups
Lima = 2⅓ cups = 6 cups
Navy = 2 cups = 6 cups

Flour
1 pound of:
White = 4 cups sifted
Whole wheat = 3½ cups stirred

Equivalent Yields

28 saltines = 1 cup crumbs
22 vanilla wafers = 1 cup crumbs
14 squares graham crackers = 1 cup crumbs
1½ slices bread = 1 cup soft crumbs
1 slice bread = ¼ cup dry crumbs
juice of 1 lemon = 3 tablespoons juice
1 pound cheese = 4 cups shredded
1 medium onion, chopped = ½ cup
12 to 14 egg yolks = 1 cup
8 to 10 egg whites = 1 cup

Ingredient Substitutions

1 cup cake flour = 1 cup **minus** 2 tablespoons all-purpose flour
1 cup self-rising flour = 1 cup sifted all-purpose flour **plus** 1¼ teaspoons baking powder **plus** a pinch of salt
1 tablespoon cornstarch = 2 tablespoons flour or 4 teaspoons quick tapioca
1 teaspoon baking powder = ¼ teaspoon soda **plus** ½ cup buttermilk (replacing ½ cup liquid)
1 cup sour milk = 1 tablespoon lemon juice or vinegar **plus** sweet milk to make 1 cup (let stand 5 minutes)
1 cup whole milk = 1 cup skim milk **plus** 2 teaspoons oil, melted margarine, or mayonnaise
1 cup light cream = ¾ cup milk **plus** ¼ cup melted margarine
1 cup yogurt = 1 cup buttermilk
1 cup sour cream = ⅓ cup margarine **plus** ¾ cup sour milk, yogurt, or buttermilk
1 clove garlic = ¼ teaspoon garlic powder
1 cup tomato juice = ½ cup tomato sauce **plus** ½ cup water
1 square (1 ounce) unsweetened chocolate = 3 tablespoons cocoa powder **plus** 1 tablespoon margarine
1 teaspoon powdered mustard = 1 tablespoon prepared mustard
1 tablespoon fresh herbs = 1 teaspoon dried herbs
1 cup light corn syrup or honey = 1¼ cups sugar (increase liquid in recipe by ¼ cup)
1 tablespoon grated raw ginger = ⅛ teaspoon ground ginger
1 cup fine dried bread crumbs = ¾ cup cracker crumbs
½ cup minced, pitted prunes or dates = ½ cup seedless raisins or currants

Can Sizes

8 ounces = 1 cup
picnic = 1¼ cups or 10½ to 12 ounces
12 ounce vacuum = 1½ cups
No. 300 = 1¾ cups or 14 to 16 ounces
No. 303 = 2 cups or 16 to 17 ounces
No. 2 = 2½ cups or 20 ounces
No. 2½ = 3½ cups or 29 ounces
No. 3 cylinder = 5¾ cups or
   46 fluid ounces
No. 10 = 12 to 13 cups or
   6 pounds, 8 ounces to
   7 pounds, 5 ounces
   (equal to 7 No. 303 cans or
   5 No. 2 cans)

Approximate Metric Conversion Factors

To convert from	to	Multiply by
Teaspoons	Milliliters	5
Tablespoons	Milliliters	15
Fluid ounces	Milliliters	30
Cups	Liters	0.24
Quarts	Liters	0.96
Milliliters	Fluid ounces	0.04
Liters	Quarts	1.04

Cooking Terms

For Preparing Ingredients:

Bread — to coat with crumbs before cooking.
Chop — to cut in pieces about the size of peas with knife, chopper, or blender.
Crush — press to extract juice with garlic press, mallet, or side of knife.
Cube — to cut in cubes ½ inch or larger.
Dice — to cut food into small cubes of uniform size (less than ½ inch).
Dredge — to sprinkle or coat with flour or other fine substance.
Grate — to cut in tiny particles using small holes of grater.
Julienne — to cut in matchlike sticks (cooked meat, cheese).
Knead — to work the dough with the heel of the hand in a pressing, folding motion.
Mince — to cut in very small pieces.
Pare — to cut off outer covering with a knife or other sharp tool.
Peel — to strip off outer covering.
Score — to cut narrow grooves or slits partway through the outer surface of food.
Shred — to cut in thin pieces using large holes on grater or shredder.
Sift — to put one or more dry ingredients through a sieve or sifter.
Sliver — to cut in long, thin pieces.
Snip — to cut in very small pieces with a scissors (parsley, chives).
Soft peaks — to beat egg whites or whipping cream until peaks are formed when beaters are lifted, but tips curl over.
Stiff peaks — to beat egg whites until peaks stand up straight when beaters are lifted, but are still moist and glossy.

Other Terms:

Baste — to moisten foods during cooking with pan drippings or special sauce to add flavor and prevent drying.
Chill — to place in refrigerator to reduce temperature.
Cool — to remove from heat and allow to come to room temperature.
Freshen fish — marinate frozen, thawed fish in milk in the refrigerator for 1 to 2 hours. Remove and cook according to recipe.
Glaze — a mixture applied to food which hardens or becomes firm and/or adds flavor and a glossy appearance.
Marinate — to allow a food to stand in a liquid to tenderize or to add flavor.

For Combining Ingredients:

(Note: These are arranged from the gentlest action to the most vigorous.)

Toss — to tumble ingredients lightly with a lifting motion (salads).

Fold — to combine ingredients lightly by a combination of two motions: one cuts vertically through mixture; the other slides the spatula or wire whisk across the bottom of the bowl and up the side, turning over (chiffon cakes, soufflés).

Cut in — to distribute solid fat in dry ingredients by chopping with knives or pastry blender.

Stir — to combine ingredients with circular or figure-8 motion until of uniform consistency.

Mix — to combine in any way that distributes all ingredients evenly.

Blend — to thoroughly combine all ingredients until very smooth and uniform.

Cream — to beat just until smooth, light, and fluffy (the combination of sugar and shortening).

Beat — to make mixture smooth by a vigorous over-and-over motion with a spoon, whip, rotary beater, or electric mixer.

Whip — to beat rapidly in order to incorporate air.

For Cooking:

Bake — to cook covered or uncovered in an oven or oven-type appliance.

Blanch — to precook in boiling water or steam to prepare foods for canning or freezing, or to loosen skin.

Boil — to heat until bubbles rise continuously and break on the surface of liquid (full rolling boil bubbles form rapidly throughout the mixture).

Braise — to cook slowly with a small amount of liquid in tightly covered pan on top of range or in the oven.

Broil — to cook by direct heat, usually in broiler, or over coals.

Brown — to cook until food changes color, usually in small amount of fat over moderate heat.

Fry — to cook in hot fat (shortening, oil, or margarine). Pan frying is to cook in small amount of fat. Deep fat frying is to cook immersed in large amount of oil or shortening.

Pan broil — to cook uncovered on hot surface, removing fat as it accumulates.

Poach — to cook in hot liquid, being careful that food holds its shape while cooking.

Roast — to cook uncovered without water added, usually in an oven.

Sauté — to brown or cook in a small amount of hot fat.

Scald — to bring to a temperature just below the boiling point where tiny bubbles form at the edge of the pan (milk).

Sear — to brown the surface of meat very quickly by intense heat.

Simmer — to cook in liquid over low heat at a temperature of 180° to 210° where bubbles form at a low rate and burst before reaching the surface.

Steam — to cook in steam with or without pressure. A small amount of boiling water is used, more water being added during steaming process if necessary.

Steep — to extract color, flavor, or other qualities from a substance by leaving it in liquid just below the boiling point.

Stew — to simmer slowly in a small amount of liquid.

Toast — to brown in oven or roaster.

Appetizers

Mock Sour Cream

- 1 cup low-fat (2%) cottage cheese
- 2 tablespoons plain low-fat yogurt
- 2 tablespoons low-fat mayonnaise

Place cottage cheese and yogurt in blender container. Process at STIR for 30 seconds, then at PUREE for 2½ minutes. Add mayonnaise and process at STIR for 30 seconds.

Yield: 1¼ cups
   ¼ cup = ½ teaspoon oil
(If regular mayonnaise is substituted for low-fat mayonnaise, ¼ cup = 1 teaspoon oil).

Spinach Dip

- 1 10-ounce package frozen chopped spinach
- 2½ cups Mock Sour Cream
- ½ cup chopped scallions
- ¼ cup finely minced parsley
- ¾ teaspoon salt
- ⅛ teaspoon pepper

Thaw spinach and squeeze out liquid. Mix spinach with remaining ingredients and chill.

Yield: 3 cups
   ¼ cup = ½ teaspoon oil

Peppery Olive Dip

- 1¼ cups Mock Sour Cream
- 1 tablespoon minced onion
- ¼ teaspoon crushed red pepper flakes
- ¼ cup chopped pimiento-stuffed olives, well drained

To Mock Sour Cream add onion, crushed pepper, and chopped olives. Combine ingredients by hand.

Yield: 1½ cups
   ¾ cup = 1 teaspoon oil

Tangy Vegetable Dip

- 3 cups Mock Sour Cream
- ¾ cup chopped green onions
- 1½ tablespoons prepared horseradish
- 1½ tablespoons Worcestershire sauce
- 1½ teaspoons caraway seed
- 1½ teaspoons celery seed
- ½ teaspoon garlic salt
- ½ teaspoon hot pepper sauce
- ½ teaspoon seasoned salt
  sliced green onions
  assorted vegetables

In large bowl, combine all ingredients except sliced green onions and assorted vegetables. Garnish with sliced green onions and chill. Serve with raw vegetables.

Yield: 3 cups
   ½ cup = 1 teaspoon oil

Mock California Dip

- 2½ cups Mock Sour Cream
- 2 tablespoons skim milk
- 1 tablespoon wine vinegar
- 2 drops hot pepper sauce
- 1 envelope dry onion soup mix

By hand, mix Mock Sour Cream with remaining ingredients. Let mixture stand in refrigerator a few hours before serving, preferably overnight.

Yield: 2½ cups
   ¼ cup = ½ teaspoon oil

Green Goddess Dip

- 2½ cups Mock Sour Cream
- 1 package Green Goddess dry salad dressing mix

Add dressing mix to Mock Sour Cream and mix well. Cover and chill overnight. Stir once before serving.

Yield: 2½ cups
   ¼ cup = ½ teaspoon oil

Curry Dip

⅔ cup low-fat mayonnaise
⅓ cup buttermilk
¾ teaspoon curry powder
¼ teaspoon salt

Combine mayonnaise and buttermilk. Add curry powder and salt. Mix until smooth. Refrigerate overnight.

Yield: 1 cup
     1 tablespoon = 1 teaspoon oil
(If regular mayonnaise is substituted for low-fat mayonnaise, 2 tablespoons = 3 teaspoons oil.)

Chili Sauce Dip

1 12-ounce bottle chili sauce
6 drops Tabasco sauce
2 tablespoons horseradish
¼ cup finely chopped celery
¼ teaspoon salt
1 tablespoon minced parsley

Combine all ingredients and chill. Serve with crisp vegetables or Snappy Tortilla Chips (see recipe).

Yield: 1½ cups

Avocado Dip

1 medium avocado, peeled and pitted
1 tablespoon buttermilk
2 tablespoons low-fat mayonnaise
1 teaspoon lemon juice
¼ teaspoon salt
¼ teaspoon hot pepper sauce

Place ingredients in blender container. Process at STIR for approximately 30 seconds until mixture is fairly smooth but yet slightly grainy in appearance. Cover and chill until served.

Yield: ⅔ cup
     ⅓ cup = 1 teaspoon oil
(If regular mayonnaise is substituted for low-fat mayonnaise, ⅓ cup = 2 teaspoons oil.)

Quick Cottage Dip

1½ cups low-fat (2%) cottage cheese
3 tablespoons plain low-fat yogurt
1½ teaspoons instant minced onion
½ teaspoon seasoned salt
1 tablespoon finely chopped canned pimiento

Place cottage cheese, yogurt, onion, and salt into a blender container. Process at BLEND until mixture is smooth. Add pimiento and stir.

Yield: 1 cup

Seven-Layer Vegetable Dip

2 cups canned red kidney beans, drained
2 tablespoons oil
1 clove garlic, mashed
1 package (1 cup) frozen guacamole, thawed
1 cup chopped green onion
1 cup peeled and chopped fresh tomato
1 cup chopped ripe olives
½ cup chopped canned green chili peppers
½ cup grated sharp cheddar cheese

In a serving dish, arrange ingredients in layers specified.
Layer 1: Mix kidney beans, oil, and garlic. Place in bottom of dish.
Layer 2: Guacamole
Layer 3: Onion
Layer 4: Tomato
Layer 5: Ripe olives
Layer 6: Chili peppers
Layer 7: Cheddar cheese
  Serve with raw vegetables or on crackers.

Yield: 6-7 cups
     ½ cup = 1 teaspoon oil

Guacamole Dip

- 2 medium avocados, peeled and pitted
- 1 medium onion, sliced
- 2 green chili peppers, chopped
- 1 tablespoon lemon juice
- 1 teaspoon salt
- ½ teaspoon ground black pepper
- 1 medium tomato, peeled and chopped
- 2 tablespoons low-fat mayonnaise

Place avocados, onion, chili peppers, lemon juice, salt, and pepper in blender. Process at LIQUIFY until onion is chopped very finely. Dip should have a slightly rough appearance when blended. Fold in tomato and low-fat mayonnaise. Refrigerate overnight to develop flavors.

Yield: 2 cups (1 serving) = 2 tablespoons
1 cup = 1 teaspoon oil
(If regular mayonnaise is substituted for low-fat mayonnaise, 1 cup = 2 teaspoons oil.)

Rainbow Relish Dip

- 1 cup low-fat (2%) cottage cheese
- 2 tablespoons low-fat yogurt
- 2 tablespoons low-fat mayonnaise
- 2 ounces cheddar cheese, grated
- 1 teaspoon cider vinegar
- 1 clove garlic, mashed
- 3 tablespoons dehydrated vegetable mixture
- ½ teaspoon horseradish

Place cottage cheese, yogurt, and cheese in blender container. Process at STIR for 30 seconds, then at PUREE for 2½ minutes. Add mayonnaise and process at STIR for 30 seconds. Add remaining ingredients to cheese mixture in blender container. Process mixture at WHIP for 30 seconds. Cover and chill overnight. Stir once before serving.

Yield: 1½ cups
¼ cups = ⅙ ounce cheese
(If regular mayonnaise is substituted for low-fat mayonnaise, ¼ cup = ½ teaspoon oil.)

Bean Dip

- ¼ cup catsup
- 1 tablespoon cider vinegar
- 1 tablespoon Worcestershire sauce
- 4 drops Tabasco sauce
- ¼ teaspoon liquid smoke
- 1 teaspoon garlic salt
- 1 teaspoon chili powder
- 1 green chili pepper, chopped
- 3 cups cooked and drained kidney beans

Place all ingredients in blender. Blend at a low speed for 10 seconds, then high speed until dip is smooth.

Yield: 3 cups

Curry Dip Variation

- 1½ cups low-fat (2%) cottage cheese
- 3 tablespoons plain low-fat yogurt
- 1 cup low-fat mayonnaise
- ¼ teaspoon turmeric
- 1 tablespoon curry powder
- ½ teaspoon garlic powder
- 2 teaspoons sugar
- ½ teaspoon salt
- 2 teaspoons lemon juice
- 2 tablespoons finely minced parsley

Place cottage cheese and yogurt in a blender container. Process at LIQUIFY until smooth. Transfer mixture to a small mixing bowl. In the order specified above and one at a time, blend remaining ingredients into puréed cottage cheese. Let mixture stand in refrigerator a few hours, preferably overnight. Serve with raw vegetables.

Yield: 2½ cups
2 tablespoons = ½ teaspoon oil
(If regular mayonnaise is substituted for low-fat mayonnaise, 2 tablespoons = 1½ teaspoons oil.)

Snappy Tortilla Chips

1 package (12) frozen tortillas, thawed
2 tablespoons margarine, melted
   salt

Lightly brush both sides of tortillas with melted margarine. Cut tortillas into pie-shaped wedges, eight per tortilla. Salt lightly. Place wedges on ungreased pan and bake at 350° for 10 minues. Remove chips from oven and cool.

Yield: 8 dozen tortilla chips
8 chips = ½ teaspoon margarine

Molded Tuna Pâté

1 4-ounce can mushroom pieces
1 envelope unflavored gelatin
½ cup boiling water
2 6½-ounce cans tuna, packed in water, drained
½ cup low-fat mayonnaise
½ cup ripe olives, pitted
¼ cup fresh parsley sprigs
¼ teaspoon salt

Into a blender container, drain liquid from mushrooms. Sprinkle gelatin over liquid and soften for a minute or until gelatin becomes clear. Add boiling water, cover blender container, and process at low speed for 10 seconds, then at high speed for 20 seconds. Add mushrooms, tuna, mayonnaise, olives, and parsley. Cover and process at medium speed for 1 minute or until tuna is finely ground, but not of puréed consistency. Pour into 4-cup mold; cover and chill for at least 3 hours. Unmold by immersing mold in hot water to rim and inverting on serving plate; serve with melba toast.

Yield: 3¼ cups pâté
½ cup = 1 ounce meat

Chicken Almond Pâté

1 double chicken breast
1 slice of medium onion
1 small raw carrot
1 celery top
½ teaspoon salt
3 peppercorns
1 bay leaf
¾ cup whole blanched almonds
2 tablespoons mayonnaise
2 tablespoons oil
2 tablespoons marsala or sherry
2 tablespoons finely minced onion
2 teaspoons Worcestershire sauce
4-5 drops Tabasco sauce
¼ teaspoon salt
⅛ teaspoon white pepper

Remove skin and fat from chicken. Boil in medium-sized saucepan with onion, carrot, celery top, salt, peppercorn, and bay leaf for 30 minutes or until meat is white throughout. Strain and reserve chicken broth as stock for future recipes. Cool and bone chicken. Grind almonds,* then chicken with food grinder set to yield finest grind possible. Reserve 2 tablespoons of ground nuts. Combine remaining ground nuts and chicken with all other ingredients. Mix well. Spray 2-cup mold with pan spray and fill with pâté. Chill for at least 3 hours. Remove pâté from mold by dipping in boiling water briefly (loosen sides with knife). Sprinkle top and dust sides with reserved almonds. Serve with saltines or Norwegian flat bread.

*Note: If grinder becomes clogged, clean it, and grind remaining almonds with chicken.

Yield: 1¼ cup pâté
2 tablespoons = ½ ounce meat
1 teaspoon oil

Chicken Canapés

- 2 cups chopped, cooked chicken breasts (approximately 2 double chicken breasts)
- ½ cup low-fat mayonnaise
- ¼ cup minced celery
- 2 tablespoons minced onion
- ¼ cup chopped pecans
- ½ teaspoon poultry seasoning
- ¼ teaspoon white pepper
- 1 teaspoon fresh lemon juice
- 1 tablespoon white cooking wine
- garlic or onion melba toast rounds
- pimiento, green pepper, or parsley

Remove skin and fat from chicken breast. Boil in medium-sized saucepan for 30 minutes or until meat is white throughout. Cool; bone and chop meat into small pieces. Mix together chicken and remaining ingredients except for melba toast and garnishes (pimiento, green pepper, or parsley). When mixing, allow meat to crumble into finer pieces. Refrigerate canapé spread for 1-3 hours. When ready to serve, spread approximately 2 teaspoons of chicken mixture on each garlic or onion round. Top with pimiento, green pepper, or parsley.

Yield: 50 appetizers
6 appetizers = 1 ounce meat
1 teaspoon oil
(If regular mayonnaise is substituted for low-fat mayonnaise, 6 appetizers = approximately 2 teaspoons oil.)

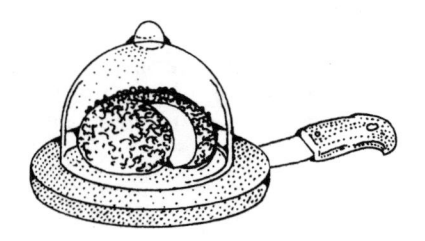

Cheese Ball

- ¼ cup water
- 1 envelope unflavored gelatin
- 1 cup (4 ounces) shredded cheddar cheese
- 2 tablespoons margarine
- 1½ cups dry curd cottage cheese
- ¼ teaspoon lemon juice
- 2½ teaspoons Worcestershire sauce
- dash cayenne pepper
- 2 tablespoons chopped, well drained pimiento
- 2 tablespoons green pepper
- 2 tablespoons dehydrated chopped onion
- 2 tablespoons chopped, well drained stuffed green olives
- ⅛ teaspoon salt
- ½ cup chopped pecans

Place water in small saucepan and sprinkle gelatin over water. Heat until gelatin dissolves. Remove saucepan from heat and cool in pan. Place in a blender container ⅓ of shredded cheese, all of margarine, cottage cheese, lemon juice, Worcestershire sauce, and cayenne pepper. Add 2-3 tablespoons of liquid gelatin. Process at a low speed for 10 seconds, medium speed for 1 minute, and high speed for 2-3 minutes, or until mixture is as smooth as cream cheese. Transfer cottage cheese mixture to small bowl. If remaining gelatin has firmed, warm over low heat until it is again a liquid. Add small amount of cottage cheese mixture to gelatin and stir well. Incorporate gelatin into remaining cottage cheese mixture and beat until smooth. Refrigerate in bowl for approximately 45 minutes. Add remaining shredded cheese, pimiento, green pepper, onion, green olives, and salt. Form into a ball, wrap in plastic wrap and refrigerate overnight. Roll in pecans and serve chilled.

Yield: 2 cups
2 tablespoons = ½ teaspoon margarine
¼ ounce cheese

Vegetable Antipasto

- 3 celery stalks, sliced into 2-inch pieces
- 3 carrots, pared, quartered lengthwise, then sliced into 2-inch pieces
- 2 medium zucchini, quartered lengthwise, then sliced into 2-inch pieces
- 1 large green pepper, sliced into approximately 1 x 1-inch cubes
- 1½ cups raw cauliflowerettes
- 1 3½-ounce can pitted black olives, drained (discard liquid)
- 10 small white onions, peeled and quartered
- ¼ pound fresh green beans, cut in half crosswise
- ¼ cup oil
- ½ cup water
- ½ cup vinegar
- 2 cloves garlic, minced
- 2 teaspoons salt
- 1 teaspoon dried oregano leaves
- ⅛ teaspoon ground black pepper

Prepare vegetables as indicated. In large saucepan, combine oil, water, vinegar, and spices. Add vegetables; stir. Over moderate heat, bring to a boil, stirring occasionally. Reduce heat; cover and simmer 5 minutes or until vegetables are crisp-tender. Cool; cover and refrigerate at least 6 hours, stirring occasionally. Drain.

Yield: 7 cups
  ½ cup = 1 teaspoon oil

Green Pepper Appetizer

- 4 large green peppers
- ⅓ cup vinegar
- ¼ cup minced onion
- ½ teaspoon salt
- ¼ teaspoon pepper
- ½ cup oil
- 1 clove garlic, crushed and minced
- ½ teaspoon dry basil
- 1 crumbled bay leaf
- 2 cups (8 ounces) shredded cheddar cheese
- ⅓ cup melted margarine
- 64 saltine cracker squares

Place peppers in a hot oven (400°F.) until skin wrinkles (10-12 minutes). Remove stems and seeds; cut into eight slices lengthwise, then halve each slice crosswise. Combine vinegar, onion, salt, pepper, oil, garlic, basil, and bay leaf in a small bowl. Add pepper slices and marinate overnight in refrigerator. Combine cheese and melted margarine in a bowl; mix well and chill. Spread crackers with ¾ teaspoon of cheese mixture. Place marinated peppers in a nearby dish and let each guest top his own cheese-covered cracker with a piece of pepper.

Yield: 64 appetizers
  1 serving = 2 crackers
    ½ teaspoon oil
    ½ teaspoon margarine
    ¼ milk equivalent

Tuna Anchovy Appetizer

- 1 7-ounce can water-packed tuna, drained
- 1 2-ounce can anchovies, drained
- ⅛ teaspoon dry mustard
- ⅛ teaspoon oregano
  few grains cayenne pepper
- 1 teaspoon lemon juice
- 1 tablespoon sweet pickle relish
- ¼ cup French salad dressing

Break tuna into bite-sized pieces. Coarsely chop anchovies and add to tuna. Add mustard, oregano, and cayenne pepper. Gently mix until spices are blended in. Add lemon juice, pickle relish, and French dressing. Mix and allow to marinate for 20 minutes or longer. Serve with melba toast or crackers.

Yield: 8 servings (2 tablespoons each)
  1 serving = 1 ounce meat
    1 teaspoon oil

Marinated Mushrooms

1 pound whole fresh mushrooms
1 package low-calorie Italian salad dressing mix
   tarragon vinegar

Wash and slice mushrooms once lengthwise. Prepare salad dressing according to package directions using tarragon vinegar. Measure ¾ cup of salad dressing and pour over mushrooms. Mix lightly. Marinate in refrigerator overnight. Drain before serving.

Yield: 60 appetizers

Pineapple and Ham Tidbits

1 16-ounce can pineapple chunks (unsweetened)
4 sprigs fresh mint
1½ pounds lean, boneless ham chunk or steak
2 tablespoons finely minced parsley

Place pineapple with its juice and mint sprigs in saucepan. Boil for 5 minutes stirring occasionally. Remove from heat, cool, and drain pineapple. Chill in refrigerator. Cut ham to same size as pineapple, (approximately ¾-inch cubes). Sprinkle pineapple with finely minced fresh parsley. Spear on frilly toothpicks (one piece of ham and one piece of pineapple). Arrange hors d'oeuvres by sticking toothpicks into a fruit or vegetable, e.g., a large tomato (bottom cut off) or grapefruit.

Yield: 40 appetizers
       2 appetizers = 1 ounce meat

Fruited Link Kabobs

1 8-ounce package imitation breakfast links, thawed
20 date halves or pitted prunes
20 canned pineapple chunks, packed in own juice, drained
10 maraschino cherries, if desired
¼ cup honey
¼ cup low-calorie French dressing

Cut breakfast links in half crosswise. On each of 10 skewers, alternate a half link, a date half, and a pineapple chunk. Repeat sequence once more for all skewers; end each skewer with a maraschino cherry. Place skewers in broiling pan. Combine honey and low-calorie French dressing. Brush kabobs with dressing mixture. Broil 5 inches from heat source for about 20 minutes or until links are evenly browned. Turn, brush second side, and continue broiling for 20 more minutes or until links are browned.

Yield: 10 kabobs

Snack Kabobs

1 package low-calorie Italian salad dressing mix
1 8-ounce package imitation breakfast links, thawed
1 medium green pepper
20 cherry tomatoes
20 fresh mushroom caps

Prepare salad dressing according to package directions. Cut breakfast links in half crosswise. Cut green pepper into approximately 20 squares. On each skewer, alternate a sausage link half, cherry tomato, chuck of green pepper, and mushroom cap. Repeat sequence once more for all skewers. Place skewers in broiling pan and brush with dressing. Broil 5 inches from heat source for about 20 minutes or until links are evenly browned. Turn, brush second side, and continue broiling for 20 more minutes or until links are browned.

Yield: 10 kabobs

Sweet-Sour Cocktail Meatballs

- 1 pound lean ground beef
- ½ cup dry bread crumbs
- ⅓ cup minced onion
- ¼ cup skim milk
- 2 egg whites
- 1 tablespoon snipped fresh parsley
- 1 teaspoon salt
- ⅛ teaspoon pepper
- ½ teaspoon Worcestershire sauce

Combine ground beef with remaining ingredients, mixing after each addition. Gently shape into ¾-inch balls. Bake at 350°F. for 30 minutes on lightly greased baking sheet. Combine with sweet-sour sauce and serve hot.

Sauce:
- 1 14-ounce can pineapple chunks in heavy syrup
- ½ cup firmly packed brown sugar
- 2 tablespoons corn starch
- 1 tablespoon instant chicken bouillon granules
- 3 tablespoons cider vinegar
- 1 tablespoon soy sauce

Pour pineapple syrup into measuring cup, and add water to equal one cup of liquid. Set aside pineapple chunks. Combine brown sugar, cornstarch, bouillon, vinegar, and soy sauce with pineapple liquid in a large heavy skillet. Over moderate heat; bring mixture to boil, stirring constantly. Boil mixture over 3 minutes. Remove from heat and stir in meatballs and pineapple chunks.

Yield: 72 meatballs
   4 meatballs = 1 ounce meat

Wakefield Specials

- 24 plain melba toast rounds
- 2 tablespoons low-fat mayonnaise
- 1 medium red onion
- ¼ cup grated Parmesan cheese
- 3 tablespoons low-fat mayonnaise

Spread each slice of melba toast with ¼ teaspoon low-fat mayonnaise. Thinly slice onion and place one thin layer of onion on each piece of toast. Mix cheese with 3 tablespoons low-fat mayonnaise. Spread cheese mixture over the onion-topped toast. Refrigerate 2-3 hours. Before serving, broil 4 inches from heat source for 4-5 minutes until puffy and slightly brown. Serve hot.

Yield: 24 appetizers
   3 appetizers = ½ teaspoon oil
(If regular mayonnaise is substituted for low-fat mayonnaise, 3 appetizers = 1 teaspoon oil.)

Appetizer Tuna Balls

- 1 7-ounce can water-packed tuna, well drained
- ½ cup fine, dry bread crumbs
- ½ teaspoon poultry seasoning
- 2 tablespoons minced onion
- 2 tablespoons minced fresh parsley
- 3 tablespoons low-fat mayonnaise
- 2 teaspoons prepared mustard
- 5 drops red pepper sauce
- 1 egg, slightly beaten
- 1 egg white, well beaten
- ½ cup crushed corn flakes

In a large bowl, flake tuna with a fork. Blend in bread crumbs, poultry seasoning, onion, parsley, low-fat mayonnaise, prepared mustard, red pepper sauce, and egg. Shape into balls, using about 2 teaspoons of tuna mixture for each. Dip balls in well-beaten egg white; roll in crushed corn flakes. Place 1 inch apart on an ungreased cookie sheet. Bake in a preheated 450°F. oven for 8-10 minutes or until hot and crisp (bake 12 minutes, if chilled). Dip in a cocktail sauce.

Tuna balls can be made ahead and chilled. Bake them just before serving.

Yield: 24 appetizer balls
   3 appetizers = approximately 1 ounce meat

Teriyaki Marinated Chicken Wings

- ¾ cup Japanese soy sauce
- 1 tablespoon white wine
- ½ cup honey or sugar
- 1 teaspoon ground ginger
- 1 whole clove garlic
- 2 pounds chicken wings
- ½ medium onion, chopped
- 1 8-ounce can pineapple chunks, packed in own juice, drained (discard juice)
- 1 medium green pepper, sliced into rings

Prepare marinade by combining soy sauce, wine, honey, ginger, and garlic. Marinate wings at least 3 hours in marinade. Remove wings and garlic from marinade; discard garlic. Bake wings in 13 x 9-inch pan at 375°F. for 30 minutes. Place onion and pineapple on top of wings; pour marinade over all. Continue baking another 30 minutes. Top with green pepper rings and bake 10 additional minutes. Drain and serve warm.

Yield: 8-10 wings
1 wing = 1 ounce meat

Marinated Teriyaki Beef

- 1 pound sirloin steak, 1 inch thick
- 2 teaspoons ground ginger
- 2 cloves garlic, minced
- 2 small onions, minced
- 2 tablespoons sugar
- ½ cup Japanese soy sauce
- ¼ cup water
- 2 tablespoons red wine

Trim fat and cut steak into ½-inch squares. To make marinade, combine remaining ingredients, reserve half for later use, pour other half over meat. Marinate for at least 2 hours or preferably overnight. Drain; discard marinade used with meat, and transfer meat to broiler pan arranged in a single layer. Broil approximately 3 inches from heat source for 5 minutes; turn meat and broil 3 minutes longer. Spear each cube with toothpick; place in heated serving dish or in chafing dish. Heat reserved marinade; pour over meat. Serve hot.

Yield: approximately 50 pieces
4 pieces = 1 ounce meat

Mushrooms Royale

- 1 pound fresh mushrooms
- 3 tablespoons margarine
- ¼ cup finely chopped green pepper
- ¼ cup finely chopped onion
- ½ teaspoon thyme
- ¼ teaspoon turmeric
- ¼ teaspoon pepper
- ½ teaspoon salt
- 1½ cups soft bread crumbs
- 5 tablespoons grated Parmesan cheese
- pan spray

Wash and detach stems from caps. Set caps aside. Trim stems and chop into medium-sized pieces. Sauté green pepper, onion, and stems in margarine for approximately 5 minutes or until tender. Remove from heat and stir in spices. Add bread crumbs and mix lightly. Coat bottom of shallow baking dish with a pan spray. Fill caps with stuffing mix and place filled side up in baking dish. Top each with approximately ¼ teaspoon Parmesan cheese. Bake 15 minutes at 350°F. Then broil 3-4 inches from heat for 2 minutes.

Yield: 30-40 appetizers
6 appetizers = 1 teaspoon margarine

Baking Mix

- 9 cups sifted all-purpose flour
- ⅓ cup baking powder
- 1 cup nonfat dry milk powder
- 4 teaspoons salt
- 1½ cup margarine

Into sifted flour, stir baking powder, dry milk, and salt. Sift all dry ingredients together until well mixed. Cut margarine into flour mixture until all particles of fat are thoroughly coated and mixture resembles coarse corn meal. Cover tightly and store in refrigerator.

Yield: 13 cups*

1 cup = 5½ teaspoons margarine

*To measure for a recipe: Do not sift. Stir lightly before measuring. Lift lightly into cup and level with spatula.

Deviled Ham Puffs

- 2 4½-ounce cans deviled ham
- 2 tablespoons chopped pecans
- 2 tablespoons minced onion
- 3 tablespoons minced stuffed green olives
- ¼ teaspoon cumin
  dash dry mustard
- 4 saltine crackers (2-inch square), finely crushed
- 3 cups Baking Mix
- ¾ cup water
  paprika

Combine first seven ingredients; mix well. To Baking Mix add water; beat 20-25 strokes until dough is stiff. Turn onto heavily floured board and knead about 15 times. Roll one-half of dough into a 12 x 10-inch rectangle. Cover half of rectangle with one-half ham mixture. Fold dough over to form a 6 x 10-inch rectangle. Cut with sharp knife into 30 rectangles, each 1 x 2 inches. Twist each gently to form a bow. Place on ungreased baking sheet and sprinkle bows with paprika. Bake in hot oven at 425°F. for 10 minutes or until golden brown. Repeat with remaining dough and ham mixture.

Yield: 60 appetizers

4 ham puffs = 1 teaspoon margarine

Pastry Cheese Balls

- 1 cup (4 ounces) grated cheddar cheese
- 3 tablespoons margarine
- ¾ cup sifted all-purpose flour
- ¼ teaspoon salt
- ¼ teaspoon paprika
- ¼ teaspoon curry powder

Mix together cheese and margarine. Sift dry ingredients together and add to cheese mixture; mix. Form dough into ¾-inch balls. Refrigerate for 2 hours. Bake at 400°F. on a lightly greased baking sheet for 12 minutes or until firm. Serve hot.

Yield: 24 appetizers

3 appetizers = 1 teaspoon margarine
½ milk equivalent

Miniature Appetizer Puffs

- 3 tablespoons margarine
- ½ cup boiling water
- ⅛ teaspoon salt
- ½ cup sifted all-purpose flour
- 1 whole large egg
- 1 large egg white

Melt margarine in boiling water; continue heating until water boils again. Lower heat, and add salt and flour all at once. Stir vigorously until dough forms a ball. Remove pan from heat; cool until bottom of pan is warm to touch. Add whole egg; stir until egg is mixed in completely. Add egg white and stir until just incorporated. Spoon dough onto lightly oiled cookie sheet using a measuring teaspoon filled approximately level. Space mounds about 1 inch apart. Bake in 450°F. oven for 10 minutes, then at 300°F. for 5-10 minutes or until puffs are desirably dry. Cool puffs on rack. When cool, put each horizontally and fill bottom with desired filling. Replace top.

Yield: 35 miniature puffs
  4 puffs = ⅛ egg
  4 puffs = 1 teaspoon margarine

Fondue

- 1 11-ounce can cheddar cheese soup
- 2 cups (8 ounces) shredded Swiss cheese
- ¼ cup white cooking wine
- ⅛ teaspoon garlic powder
  French bread

In a medium-sized pan over very low heat, stir together soup and cheese for 10-15 minutes or until cheese melts. Stir in wine and garlic powder. Transfer to fondue pot and serve with cubes of French bread.

Yield: 2 cups
  ¼ cup = 1 ounce cheese

Italian Nuts and Bolts

- 1½ cups circle-shaped oat cereal
- 1½ cups bite-sized shredded wheat
- ½ cup slivered almonds
- ½ cup peanuts
- 2 tablespoons margarine, melted
- 2½ teaspoons Italian seasoning
- ½ teaspoon garlic powder
- ½ teaspoon onion salt
- ¼ cup grated Parmesan cheese

In a large bowl, stir together oat circles, shredded wheat, almonds, and peanuts. Combine melted margarine, Italian seasoning, garlic powder, and onion salt; dribble over cereal mixture and blend well. Spread mixture in a single layer on a rimmed baking sheet. Sprinkle with Parmesan cheese. Bake at 250°F. for 45 minutes or until lightly toasted. Stir several times during baking period. Cool.

Yield: 4 cups
  ⅔ cup = 1 teaspoon margarine

Candied Almonds

- ½ cup boiling water
- 1 cup sugar
- ⅛ teaspoon cream of tartar
- 2 cups whole blanched almonds

Place boiling water in small sauce pan. Add sugar and cream of tartar, being careful not to leave any sugar on sides of pan. Slowly bring to a boil, making sure all sugar is completely dissolved before boiling begins. Boil over high heat. Add almonds when candy thermometer registers 225°F. Continue to heat while stirring, until 320°F. is reached. Remove pan from heat source. Stir nut-syrup mixture until it becomes thick and sticky. Spoon mass onto a lightly greased pan and quickly separate nuts. Allow to cool.

Yield: approximately 225 nuts

Soups

Manhattan Clam Chowder

- 3 7-ounce cans minced clams
- 3 medium potatoes, peeled and diced
- 3 medium carrots, peeled and diced
- 4 medium stalks celery, chopped
- 1 16-ounce can tomatoes, undrained
- 1 tablespoon bacon-flavored bits
- 2 teaspoons salt
- ½ teaspoon thyme leaves
- ¼ teaspoon pepper
- 1 6-ounce can tomato paste

In a large kettle or Dutch oven, combine all ingredients, except tomato paste, with 4 cups of water. Cover and simmer for 45 minutes. Stir in tomato paste and simmer another 15 minutes.

Yield: 10 cups
1 cup = 2 ounces meat

Salmon Soup

- 1 cup canned salmon
  skim milk
- 1 10¾-ounce can tomato soup
- ¾ cup cream style corn
- ¼ teaspoon curry powder
- ¼ teaspoon ground ginger
- 1 tablespoon parsley flakes

Drain salmon, reserving liquid. Flake the salmon and place in medium sized saucepan. Add enough milk to the reserved liquid to make 1 cup. Blend this with the soup in a small bowl. Add corn, curry powder, ginger, and parsley. Add this to the saucepan and heat.

Yield: 4 servings (1 cup each)
1 serving = 2 ounces meat

New England Clam Chowder

- ¾ cup chopped onion
- 1 tablespoon margarine
- 2 cups cubed raw potatoes
- 1 teaspoon salt
- 1 teaspoon bacon-flavored bits
  dash of pepper
- 1 cup water
- 2 7-ounce cans minced clams
- 1 cup evaporated skim milk

In large saucepan, cook onion in margarine until tender. Add potatoes, salt, bacon-flavored bits, pepper, and water. Cover and simmer 20-30 minutes or until potatoes are tender. Stir in clams and milk. Heat (do not boil).

Yield: 4 servings (1 cup each)
1 cup = 3½ ounces meat

Lobster Bisque

- 2 11¼-ounce cans condensed green pea soup
- 2 11-ounce cans condensed bisque of tomato soup
- 2 13-ounce cans evaporated skim milk
- ½ teaspoon pepper
- 1 teaspoon Worcestershire sauce
- 2 5-ounce cans lobster meat, drained and broken apart
- ⅓ cup dry sherry

Combine all ingredients except lobster meat and sherry in large saucepan. Beat with rotary beater for 1 minute and heat. Stir in lobster meat and sherry; heat to serving temperature.

Yield: 10 servings (1 cup each)
1 serving = 1 ounce meat

Fish Stew

- 2 pounds fish fillets (turbot, halibut, etc.)
- 2 tablespoons plus 2 teaspoons oil
- ½ cup chopped onion
- 1 clove garlic, minced
- ¼ cup chopped green pepper
- 3 stalks celery, sliced
- 3 carrots, cut julienne-style
- 1 28-ounce can tomatoes
- 1 cup water
- 2 chicken bouillon cubes
- ¼ teaspoon thyme
- 1 teaspoon salt
- ⅛ teaspoon pepper
- ¼ teaspoon basil
- 2 tablespoons dry parsley

Cut fish into 1 inch-square pieces. Sauté onion, garlic, green pepper, celery, and carrots in oil for 3 minutes. Add tomatoes with liquid from can, water, bouillon cubes, and all seasonings, except 1 tablespoon of parsley. Cover and simmer 10-15 minutes or until vegetables are crisp-tender. Add the 1-inch fillet pieces. Cover and simmer an additional 5-10 minutes or until the fish flakes easily. Sprinkle with remaining parsley.

Yield: 8 servings (1 cup each)
1 serving = 3 ounces meat
1 teaspoon oil

American Style Bouillabaisse

- 1 clove garlic, minced
- 1 large onion, finely chopped or grated
- 2 tablespoons oil
- 1 cup dry white or red wine
- 1 7-ounce can minced clams
- 1 6-ounce bottle clam juice
- 1 46-ounce can tomato sauce
- 1 tablespoon dried oregano, crushed
- 1 tablespoon dried basil, crushed
- 2 pounds sole, haddock, or cod pinch of saffron (optional)
- 1 small red chili pepper, crushed or minced
- 1 teaspoon hot pepper sauce

Place the vegetable oil in a large pot. Lightly cook the onion and garlic until clear and golden. Add clams, clam juice, wine, saffron, and hot pepper, and simmer for 20 minutes. Add tomato juice, sauce, and herbs, and cook over low heat for another 20 minutes. Cut fish into spoon-size pieces and add to the hot broth, then heat for another 20 minutes. Serve in a warmed bowl with a sprinkling of minced parsley. (For a variation, add 1 package of frozen okra or a can of cut okra 10 minutes after adding the fish.)

Yield: 10 servings (1 cup each)
1 serving = 2½ ounces meat
½ teaspoon oil

Gazpacho (Cold Mexican Soup)

- 4 cups tomato juice
- ½ medium yellow onion, peeled and coarsely chopped
- 1 small green pepper, chopped
- 1 small cucumber, pared and chopped
- 1 4-ounce can peeled green chilies, seeded, chopped (optional)
- 1½ teaspoons Worcestershire sauce
- 1 clove garlic, minced
- 1 drop Tabasco sauce (optional)
- ¾ teaspoon seasoning salt
- ¼ teaspoon freshly ground black pepper
- 2 tablespoons oil
- 1 large tomato, finely diced
- 2 tablespoons minced chives or green onion tops
- 1 lemon cut in 8 wedges

Put 2 cups of tomato juice and all other ingredients except diced tomato, chives, and lemon wedges in the blender. Blend until well puréed. Slowly add the remaining 2 cups of tomato juice to the blender. Pour the mixture into a large bowl, and add the chopped tomato. Garnish with the chopped chives, and serve with the lemon wedges.

Yield: 6 servings (1 cup each)
1 serving = 1 teaspoon oil

Po-mato Bisque

- 2 large yellow onions, peeled and thinly sliced
- 3 tablespoons margarine
- 6 cups sliced, peeled fresh tomatoes (or 3½ cups canned tomatoes)
- 3 cups thinly sliced, pared raw Idaho potatoes
- 6 cups water
- 2 tablespoons beef bouillon granules
- 2 teaspoons sugar
- 1½ teaspoons salt
- ½ teaspoon paprika
- ½ teaspoon basil leaves, crushed
- 2 cups skim milk

Sauté onions in margarine for 5-10 minutes or until tender. Add tomatoes and simmer 20 minutes, covered. Add potatoes, water, beef bouillon granules, sugar, salt, paprika, and basil. Cook, covered, for 30-40 minutes or until potatoes are tender. Cool soup until tepid, then put in blender and pureé. Add milk and gently heat, stirring continuously. Do not boil.

Yield: 8 servings (1¾ cups each)
1 serving = ¼ cup milk
1 teaspoon margarine

Cold Chicken Consommé

- 2 cups chicken consommé, cold
- 1 medium carrot, pared and shredded
- 1 green onion top, minced
- 1 hard-boiled egg, coarsely chopped
- ½ teaspoon lemon juice
- 4 teaspoons fresh minced parsley

Mix consommé with shredded carrots, minced green onion tops, chopped hard-boiled egg, and lemon juice. Put in 4 chilled cups or icers, and sprinkle top with parsley.

Yield: 4 servings (1 cup each)
1 serving = ¼ egg

Vichyssoise

- 5 green onions, chopped (use white part only)
- ⅓ cup chopped onion
- 1 tablespoon margarine
- 2 cups diced (½-inch cubes) raw potatoes
- 3 cups chicken stock, fat skimmed (or chicken bouillon)
- 1 13-ounce can evaporated skim milk
- ⅛ teaspoon ground black pepper
- fluid skim milk, if necessary

In a 2-quart saucepan, sauté onions in margarine about 5 minutes or until soft (do not brown). Add potatoes and chicken stock; boil gently (uncovered) 30-40 minutes or until potatoes are very tender.

Blend soup using blender or mixer until creamy white and very smooth. Add evaporated skim milk and pepper, blend thoroughly. If thinner consistency is desired, blend in small amount of fluid skim milk.

Serve hot or cold.* Garnish with chives, parsley, dill, paprika, or watercress.

*After chilling, soup may need to be thinned with additional fluid skim milk.

Yield: 6 servings (1 cup each)
1 serving = ½ teaspoon margarine

Matzo Balls

- ½ cup matzo meal
- ½ teaspoon salt
- 2 whole eggs
- 2 tablespoons cooked marrow*
- ½ teaspoon chopped fresh parsley

Mix these ingredients together. Refrigerate until firm enough to form into balls (at least 60 minutes). Drop into boiling liquid (salted water or soup) and simmer 15-20 minutes until cooked.

*To cook marrow, poach gently in the bone in just enough water to cover, or roast in a 350°F. oven for about 1 hour.

Yield: 10 matzo balls
1 matzo ball = ⅕ of one egg

Salads & Dressings

Broccoli and Cauliflower Salad

- 1 pound fresh cauliflower, chopped or broken into small flowerettes
- 1 pound fresh broccoli, chopped
- 1 small onion, chopped
- ⅓ cup vinegar
- ½ cup sugar
- ⅔ cup mayonnaise-type salad dressing
- 1 teaspoon salt

Combine cauliflower, broccoli, and onion; toss well. Combine remaining ingredients, mixing well; pour over vegetables. Let stand in refrigerator overnight.

Yield: 8 servings
1 serving = 2 teaspoons oil

Marinated Carrots

- 4 pounds raw carrots, sliced
- 1 medium onion, thinly sliced
- 1 green pepper, chopped
- ½ cup water
- 1 can tomato soup
- 1 cup vinegar
- ¾ cup sugar
- 1 teaspoon prepared mustard
- 1 teaspoon Worcestershire sauce
- 1 teaspoon mustard seed
- 1 teaspoon celery seed
- salt and pepper to taste

Cook carrots until tender, but not soft. Drain. Layer carrots, onion, and green pepper in a serving dish. Combine remaining ingredients and mix well. Pour over carrots. Marinate in refrigerator for at least 24 hours. Carrots will keep for up to ten days.

Yield: 12 cups (24 ½-cup servings)

Crunchy Cabbage Salad

- 4 cups shredded Chinese cabbage*
- ½ cup sliced fresh mushrooms
- ½ cup drained, sliced water chestnuts
- 1 tablespoon chopped green onion
- ⅓ cup mayonnaise-type salad dressing
- 2 tablespoons soy sauce
- ⅓ cup toasted almonds (optional)

In large bowl, combine cabbage, chestnuts, mushrooms, and onion. In small bowl combine salad dressing and soy sauce. Pour over cabbage mixture and toss lightly. Just before serving, add almonds and toss lightly. Serve immediately.

*If Chinese cabbage is not available, head cabbage may be substituted.

Yield: 4 servings (1 cup each)
1 serving = 1½ teaspoons oil

Fresh Mushroom Salad

- 1-1½ pounds fresh mushrooms, sliced
- 1 tablespoon chopped fresh parsley
- 2 tablespoons lemon juice
- 1 teaspoon mustard (prepared or dry)
- 1 teaspoon salt
- 1 teaspoon horseradish
- ¼ teaspoon oregano leaves
- ⅛ teaspoon ground black pepper
- ¼ cup finely chopped celery
- ½ cup chopped onion
- ¼ cup mayonnaise-type salad dressing
- ½ cup sour cream

Mix all ingredients well except mushrooms. Stir in sliced mushrooms.

Yield: 6 servings (⅔ cup each)
1 serving = ½ dairy equivalent
1 teaspoon oil

Curried Spinach Salad

Salad:
- 1 pound fresh spinach, torn into bite-sized pieces
- 1 medium Delicious apple, chopped
- 1/3 cup dry roasted peanuts
- 1/4 cup raisins
- 2½ tablespoons thin-sliced green onions
- 1 tablespoon toasted sesame seeds

Dressing:
- 3 tablespoons white wine vinegar
- 3 tablespoons oil
- 1 teaspoon finely chopped chutney
- 1/4 teaspoon curry powder
- 1/4 teaspoon salt
- 1/4 teaspoon dry mustard
- 1/16 teaspoon liquid hot pepper seasoning

Mix salad dressing ingredients together and keep at room temperature for 2 hours before serving. Pour over combined salad ingredients and toss.

Yield: 6 servings
1 serving = 1½ teaspoons oil

Crunchy Topping for Salad

- 2 cups oats (quick or old-fashioned), uncooked
- 1/4 cup margarine, melted
- 1/3 cup grated Parmesan cheese
- 1/3 cup wheat germ or unprocessed bran
- 1/4 teaspoon onion or garlic salt

Combine all ingredients; mix well. Bake on ungreased low-sided cookie sheet in preheated 350°F. oven for 15-18 minutes or until golden brown. Turn the mixture a few times while baking.

Cool; store in tightly covered container in refrigerator for up to three months. Sprinkle over tossed green salads, soups, casseroles, or vegetables.

For variation, add 1 teaspoon oregano and 1/2 teaspoon thyme to mixture before baking.

Yield: 2⅔ cups
1 tablespoon = 1/3 teaspoon margarine

Molded Vegetable Salad

- 1 cup shredded green cabbage
- 1 cup grated carrots
- 3/4 cup sliced celery
- 1/2 bunch green onion, chopped
- 1/4 cup chopped green pepper
- 1 tablespoon sugar
- 1/4 cup wine vinegar
- 1/4 cup cold water
- 4 tablespoons (4 envelopes) unflavored gelatin
- 2½ cups tomato juice
- 2 tablespoons lemon juice
- 1 tablespoon grated onion
- 1/2 teaspoon salt
- 1/4 teaspoon dry mustard
- ground black pepper

Marinate vegetables in sugar and vinegar at least 1 hour. Soften gelatin in cold water; add heated tomato juice, and stir until gelatin is dissolved. Chill until syrupy. Drain vegetables well; add to tomato mixture along with lemon juice, onion, salt, mustard, and pepper (to taste). Pour into 1½-quart mold and chill until firm.

Yield: approximately 6 cups
(12 ½-cup servings)

Herbed Tomato Slices

- 4 medium tomatoes
- 1 red onion
- 1 clove garlic, minced
- 1 teaspoon oregano
- 1/2 teaspoon salt
- 1/4 cup wine vinegar
- 2 tablespoons oil
- 1/2 cup chopped green onion

Cut both the tomatoes and the red onion into thin slices. Place in a plastic bag with minced garlic, oregano, salt, vinegar, and oil. Seal well. Marinate 2-3 hours, turning once or twice to coat well. To serve, remove from marinade, arrange on a plate, and sprinkle with chopped green onion.

Yield: 6 servings
1 serving = 1 teaspoon oil

Gazpacho Salad

- 4 tomatoes, peeled and sliced
- 2 Italian or Bermuda onions, peeled and thinly sliced
- 2 cucumbers, thinly sliced
- 2 stalks celery, thinly sliced
- ½-¾ cup fine, dry, seasoned bread crumbs
- ½ cup Garlic French Dressing watercress or lettuce (optional)

Place alternate layers of vegetables in a glass bowl. Sprinkle with bread crumbs. Chill for at least 1 hour. Pour dressing over all and toss at table. Serve on watercress or lettuce, if desired.

Yield: 8 cups

Garlic French Dressing

- 1 small clove garlic, crushed
- ½ teaspoon freshly ground black pepper
- ¾ teaspoon salt
- ¼ cup vinegar
- ¾ cup oil

Mix all ingredients in a jar and shake well before using.

Yield: 1 cup
  1 tablespoon = 2¼ teaspoons oil

Sweet-Sour Dressing

- ¼ cup instant nonfat dry milk powder
- 3 tablespoons sugar
- 1½ teaspoons salt
- 1½ teaspoons dry mustard
- ⅓ cup water
- 2 cups oil
- ½ cup vinegar

Combine first five ingredients in deep bowl. Beat with mixer until thoroughly mixed. Add oil, ¼ cup at a time. Beat after each addition until oil is blended and mixture is smooth. Add vinegar all at once, and beat until smooth and thick. Stir or shake well after overnight refrigeration.

Yield: 3 cups
  1 tablespoon = 1 teaspoon oil

Catalina Salad Dressing

- 1½ cups oil
- ½ cup vinegar
- ½ cup catsup
- 1½ cups sugar
- ½ teaspoon salt
- ½ teaspoon paprika
- 1½ teaspoons celery seed
- 1 small onion, grated

Mix all ingredients together in a blender until thick and smooth.

Yield: 4 cups
  1 tablespoon = 1 teaspoon oil

Celery Seed Dressing

- ⅔ cup sugar
- 1 teaspoon dry mustard
- 1 teaspoon paprika
- 1 teaspoon celery seed
- ¼ teaspoon salt
- ⅓ cup honey
- ⅓ cup vinegar
- 1 tablespoon lemon juice
- 1 teaspoon grated onion
- 1 cup oil

Mix all dry ingredients. Blend in honey, vinegar, lemon juice, and onion. Add oil in slow stream, beating constantly with electric mixer, until thick. Stir or shake well after overnight refrigeration.

Yield: 2 cups
  1 tablespoon = 1½ teaspoons oil

Creamy Garlic Dressing

- 1 cup low-fat (2%) cottage cheese
- ½ cup finely minced onion
  dash Worcestershire sauce
  dash Tabasco sauce
- 1 clove garlic, finely minced (to taste)
  fresh ground black pepper (to taste)
  skim milk

In blender, blend first six ingredients until smooth. Add skim milk to thin to desired consistency. Refrigerate, preferably overnight. May be used as a dip by omitting skim milk.

Yield: 1½ cups

Meat

Stir-Fried Beef and Vegetables

- 3 tablespoons soy sauce
- 2 tablespoons cooking sherry
- ¼ teaspoon sugar
- ⅛ teaspoon ground ginger
- 1 pound boneless round steak, fat trimmed, cut into strips ¼ by 1½ inches
- 3 tablespoons oil, divided
- 2 medium onions, each cut into 8 wedge-shaped pieces
- 2 stalks celery, cut on the diagonal into ¼-inch slices
- 2 small green peppers, seeded, cut into ⅛-inch slices lengthwise
- 1 8-ounce can water chestnuts, drained, cut into ⅛-inch slices
- 1 4-ounce can mushroom pieces, drained
- ½ teaspoon salt

In a medium-sized bowl, combine soy sauce, sherry, sugar, and ginger. Marinate beef slices in mixture while preparing vegetables. In a large-sized skillet, heat 2 tablespoons oil. Stir-fry onions, 2 minutes over medium-high heat; add celery, cook 1 additional minute. Add green peppers, water chestnuts, mushroom pieces, and salt; cook 2 more minutes or until green pepper is crisp-tender. Transfer vegetable mixture to a warm bowl. Add 1 more tablespoon oil to skillet. Stir-fry meat in oil about 2 minutes or until meat loses its pink color. Return vegetables to skillet; cook until mixture is hot. Transfer to a warm serving dish. Serve over rice.

Yield: 4 servings (1½ cups each)
1 serving = 2 teaspoons oil
3 ounces meat

Summer Garden Stir-Fry

- 1 pound lean ground beef
- 2 cloves garlic, minced
- 1 tablespoon margarine
- 1 medium yellow onion, cut into ⅛-inch slices
- ½ large carrot, cut into paper-thin rounds
- 1 medium stalk celery, cut on the diagonal into ¼-inch slices
- 1 teaspoon salt
- ½ teaspoon ground black pepper
- ½ medium head iceberg lettuce, chopped
- ½ medium zucchini squash, cut into ¼-inch slices
- 1½ cups cherry tomatoes, halved
- ½ large green pepper, cut into ¼-inch strips
- 2 teaspoons soy sauce

In a large skillet, brown ground beef with garlic; remove from pan, drain on paper towels. In a clean pan, melt margarine. Sauté onion, carrot, and celery over high heat 2-3 minutes or until onion softens. Lower heat to medium; add salt and pepper; cook mixture, covered, for 6-8 minutes or until carrots are almost crisp-tender. Add chopped lettuce, zucchini, cherry tomatoes, and green pepper. Cook, covered, stirring occasionally for about 5 minutes or until tomatoes are tender. Before serving, add 2 teaspoons soy sauce, and return ground beef to skillet; toss. Heat mixture through. Serve over hot rice.

Yield: 4 servings (1½ cups each)
1 serving = 3 ounces meat

Pepper Steak

1½ pounds sirloin steak (½ inch thick)
4 tablespoons margarine
½ teaspoon salt
½ teaspoon ginger
1 clove garlic, minced
1 cup beef broth
4 tablespoons soy sauce
2 medium onions, cut into 8 pieces
2 green peppers, cut in ½-inch strips
2 tablespoons cornstarch
¼ cup cold water
2 tomatoes, peeled, cut into 8 pieces
3-4 cups hot cooked rice

Cut meat into strips. Melt margarine in large skillet. Brown meat thoroughly on both sides. Push meat to one side of pan. Stir in broth, soy sauce, garlic, salt, and ginger. Cover and simmer 5 minutes or until meat is tender. Blend cornstarch and water; stir gradually into meat mixture. Cook, stirring constantly, until mixture thickens and boils. Boil and stir 1 minute. Add green peppers and onions. Cover, simmer 3 minutes, add tomatoes and heat through. Serve over rice.

Yield: 4 servings
      1 serving = 6 ounces meat
                     3 teaspoons margarine

Beef Roast in Beer

3-4 pounds boneless beef rump roast, fat trimmed
    salt
    pepper
1 medium yellow onion, sliced
¼ cup chili sauce
2 tablespoons brown sugar
1 clove garlic, minced
1 12-ounce can beer, room temperature

Season roast with salt and pepper. Place meat in a 13 x 9 x 2-inch pan; cover with onion slices. In a small bowl, mix together chili sauce, brown sugar, garlic, and beer. Pour mixture over meat. Cover with aluminum foil, and bake in a preheated 350°F. oven about 2 hours. Uncover and bake 30 minutes more, basting occasionally with jucies. To serve, carve meat across the grain.

Yield: 8 servings
      1 serving = approximately 4 ounces meat

Beef Parmigiana

1½ pounds round steak, trimmed
3 tablespoons all-purpose flour
⅛ teaspoon ground black pepper
⅓ cup seasoned bread crumbs
½ cup grated Parmesan cheese
½ teaspoon crushed basil
1 whole egg, slightly beaten
1 tablespoon water
1 tablespoon oil
1 15-ounce can tomato sauce
1 clove garlic
1 teaspoon sugar
½ teaspoon ground oregano
4 ounces mozzarella cheese, sliced
    oregano

Cut steak into six portions. In a small bowl, mix together flour and pepper. Dredge meat in flour mixture. Pound with mallet or with dull edge of large knife to tenderize meat. In separate bowl, combine bread crumbs, Parmesan cheese, and basil; in another bowl, combine the egg and water. Dip meat in egg mixture, then in crumb mixture, coating evenly. Place coated meat in ungreased 13 x 9 x 2-inch pan. In large bowl, mix together oil, tomato sauce, garlic, sugar, and ½ teaspoon oregano. Pour over meat. Cover pan with foil, sealing edges. Bake in preheated 375°F. oven for 45-55 minutes or until meat is tender. Top each serving of meat with a slice of mozzarella cheese; sprinkle very lightly with oregano. Bake, uncovered, 5 minutes more.

Yield: 6 servings
      1 serving = 3 ounces meat
                     ½ teaspoon oil
                     ⅔ dairy equivalent
                     ⅙ egg

Mushroom Beef

- 3 pounds beef stew meat, cut into 1-inch cubes, fat trimmed
- 1 pound fresh mushrooms, halved
- 1 package dry onion soup mix
- 1 10½-ounce can golden mushroom soup, undiluted
- 1 cup cooking sherry
- 2 cloves garlic, minced
- ⅛ teaspoon ground black pepper
- 3 tablespoons quick-cooking tapioca

In a Dutch oven, combine all ingredients; cover. (For this recipe, there is no need to brown meat cubes first.) Bake in a preheated 325°F. oven about 2½ hours or until meat is tender. Serve over rice or noodles.

Or: Mix in a slow-cooking pot. Cover and cook 8 hours on low setting, then 1 hour on high setting or until meat is tender. Stir once or twice while cooking on high. Serve over rice or noodles.

Yield: 8 servings (1 cup each)
1 serving = 4 ounces meat

South-of-the-Border Beef Strips

- 2 pounds boneless round steak, fat trimmed, cut into ½-inch strips
- ⅛ teaspoon garlic powder
- ¼ teaspoon ground black pepper
- ½ teaspoon salt
- 1 tablespoon chili powder
- 1 tablespoon powdered mustard
- 1 cup coarsely chopped onion
- 1 teaspoon beef instant bouillon granules
- 1 16-ounce can tomatoes, cut up, with liquid
- 1 16-ounce can kidney beans, drained

Place meat in bottom of slow-cooking pot. In a medium-sized bowl, mix together remaining ingredients except for beans. Pour over meat, cover and cook for 6-8 hours on low setting. Add beans; cook, covered, on high for 30 minutes.

Serve, using slotted spoon, over rice or noodles.

Yield: 6 servings (1 cup each)
1 serving = 4 ounces meat

Round Steak Casserole

- 2 pounds round steak, fat trimmed, cut into 6 pieces
- ¼ teaspoon garlic powder
- ½ teaspoon salt
- ¼ teaspoon ground black pepper
- 1 large yellow onion, sliced into rings
- 4 medium baking (Idaho) potatoes, pared and cut into 1-inch cubes
- 1 16-ounce can French-style green beans, undrained
- 1 10¾-ounce can tomato soup, undiluted
- 1 16-ounce can tomatoes, undrained

Place ingredients in slow-cooker in order given and stir lightly. Cover and cook on low setting for approximately 8-9 hours or until meat is tender and potatoes can be pierced with a fork. Stir before serving.

Yield: 6 servings
1 serving = 4 ounces meat

Savory Beef Stew

- 1 pound lean chuck cubes
- 2 tablespoons oil
- salt
- pepper
- 2 large carrots, coarsely chopped
- 3 medium onions, coarsely chopped
- 6 medium potatoes, pared and cut into ½-inch cubes
- 2 stalks celery, coarsely chopped
- 3 teaspoons beef bouillon granules
- 1 10-ounce package frozen peas

Brown meat in oil. Put into pan with salt, pepper, and 1 quart of boiling water. Simmer meat for one hour. Replace water that has boiled away, and continue to simmer for 30 minutes. Add carrots and onion, and continue to simmer for 30 minutes. Add potatoes and celery, continue cooking for 30 minutes. Add and dissolve bouillon cubes. Add peas and simmer for another 30 minutes. Add salt and pepper to taste.

Yield: 4 servings
      1 serving = 3 ounces meat
                   1½ teaspoons oil

Barbecued Pot Roast

- 3 pounds beef pot roast, fat trimmed
- 2 teaspoons salt
- ¼ teaspoon pepper
- 2 tablespoons oil
- ⅓ cup water
- 1 8-ounce can tomato sauce
- 3 medium yellow onions, coarsely chopped
- 2 cloves garlic, crushed
- ½ cup catsup
- 2 tablespoons lemon juice
- 2 tablespoons vinegar
- 3 tablespoons brown sugar
- 1 teaspoon powdered mustard
- 3 tablespoons Worcestershire sauce
- 1-3 drops Tabasco sauce (optional)

Season roast with salt and pepper. Brown well in oil using Dutch oven; add water, tomato sauce, onions, and garlic. Cover and simmer 2-3 hours or until meat is ready to fall apart. Cool meat slightly; remove any remaining fat and bone. Shred meat with fingers or with fork and return to Dutch oven. Stir in remaining ingredients; simmer uncovered for 1-2 hours more or until sauce has been condensed sufficiently for serving. Serve over hamburger buns.

Yield: 8 servings
      1 serving = 4 ounces meat
                   ¾ teaspoon oil

Piquant Beef

- 2 tablespoons oil
- 1¼ pounds flank or round steak, fat trimmed, cut across grain into ¼-inch thick strips
- ½ cup coarsely chopped onion
- 1 small clove garlic, crushed
- 2 2½-ounce cans sliced mushrooms, drained
- 1 10¾-ounce can tomato soup, undiluted
- 1 cup buttermilk
- 6-8 drops red pepper sauce
- 1 tablespoon Worcestershire sauce
- ½ teaspoon salt
- ⅛ teaspoon ground black pepper
- ½ teaspoon ground oregano*
- 2 tablespoons flour
- ¼ cup cold water

*For a very good variation, substitute ¼ teaspoon dill weed.

Heat oil in large skillet; add meat, onion, and garlic. Cook until meat is well browned. In a medium-sized bowl, combine mushrooms, tomato soup, buttermilk, red pepper, and Worcestershire sauce, and spices; pour over meat. Cover and simmer for 60 minutes or until meat is tender. With a fork, blend flour and water together and add slowly to beef mixture, stirring continuously. Cook until smooth and thickened.

Serve over cooked rice or pasta.

Yield: 4 servings (1 cup each)
      1 serving = 4 ounces meat
                   1½ teaspoons oil

Bavarian Dinner

- 1 pound stew beef, fat trimmed
- 1 large yellow onion, sliced
- 2 tablespoons oil
- 1½ cups water
- 1½ teaspoons salt
- ⅛ teaspoon ground black pepper
- ¾ teaspoon caraway seeds
- 1 bay leaf
- ¼ cup white vinegar
- 1 tablespoon sugar
- ½ small head red cabbage, cut into 4 wedges
- additional water, if necessary
- ¼ cup gingersnap crumbs (crushed gingersnaps)

In a Dutch oven, brown meat and onion in oil until onion is golden. Add water, salt, pepper, caraway seeds, and bay leaf. Reduce heat, cover and simmer 1¼ hours. Add vinegar and sugar; mix. Place cabbage wedges on top of meat. Cover and simmer 45 minutes more. Arrange meat and cabbage in a platter and keep warm. Strain drippings and skim off fat. Add enough water to drippings to yield 1 cup liquid. Return liquid to Dutch oven with gingersnap crumbs. Stir and heat to boiling. Boil 1 minute: Pour gravy over meat and serve.

Yield: 4 servings
1 serving = 3 ounces meat
1½ teaspoons oil

Hamburger Stew

- 1½ pounds lean ground beef
- 6 cups water
- 2 teaspoons instant beef bouillon granules
- ½ cup long grain rice, uncooked
- 12 cups coarsely chopped raw cabbage (about 1½ medium heads)
- 4 large carrots, pared and cut into ⅛-inch slices
- 3 ribs celery, coarsely chopped
- 2 teaspoons salt
- ¼ teaspoon ground black pepper
- 2 tablespoons finely chopped green pepper

In a Dutch oven, brown beef; drain on paper towels. Pour off excess fat and return beef to Dutch oven. Add remaining ingredients except for green pepper, and mix well. Bring to a boil, reduce heat and simmer, covered, 35 minutes, stirring occasionally. Add green pepper and simmer an additional 5 minutes.

Yield: 7 servings (2 cups each)
1 serving = 2½ ounces meat

Souper Supper

- 1 pound lean ground beef
- 1 large yellow onion, coarsely chopped
- 1 16-ounce can cut green beans, drained
- 1 10¾-ounce can tomato soup, undiluted
- ¼ teaspoon ground black pepper
- 3 cups mashed potatoes, mashed without fat or milk (approximately 3 large potatoes)
- ½ teaspoon salt
- ¼ teaspoon baking soda
- 2 whole eggs, well beaten
- ½ cup buttermilk
- 1 tablespoon grated Parmesan cheese

In a large-sized skillet, brown ground beef and onion. Stir in green beans, tomato soup, and black pepper. Transfer to a lightly oiled 2-quart casserole dish. Make a topping by mixing together mashed potatoes, salt, and soda. (Color of mashed potatoes may temporarily darken, but will return to normal upon addition of buttermilk.) Combine eggs and buttermilk. Mix well and stir into mashed potatoes. Spread on top of ground beef mixture. Sprinkle Parmesan cheese over top of potatoes. Bake, uncovered, in a preheated 375°F. oven for 20-25 minutes or until top is lightly browned.

Yield: 4 servings (2 cups each)
1 serving = 3 ounces meat

Beef and Rice Party Casserole

- 4 cups water
- 2 teaspoons beef instant bouillon granules
- 1⅓ cups uncooked long grain white rice
- 2 10¾-ounce cans cream of celery soup, undiluted
- 1 4-ounce can mushroom pieces, undrained
- ½ cup water
- ½ cup white cooking wine
- 2 teaspoons instant beef bouillon granules
- 1 teaspoon Worcestershire sauce
- 1 bay leaf, finely crumbled
- ¼ teaspoon ground thyme
- ¾-1 teaspoon ground black pepper
- ½ teaspoon paprika
- 1 medium yellow onion, finely chopped
- 1 clove garlic, minced
- 2 tablespoons oil
- 2 pounds lean ground beef
- ¼ cup finely chopped fresh parsley

Combine water and beef bouillon granules in a covered medium-sized saucepan and bring to a boil. Remove pan from heat; add rice and allow to stand 15 minutes, covered. In a 3-quart casserole (must have cover), mix together soup, mushroom pieces with liquid, water, wine, beef bouillon granules, Worcestershire sauce, bay leaf, thyme, black pepper, and paprika. Drain rice after it has soaked 15 minutes and add to casserole; stir. In a large skillet over medium heat, sauté onion and garlic in oil until golden; add to casserole. In same skillet, brown ground beef. Drain on paper towels. Add beef to casserole dish and mix thoroughly; cover. (At this point, casserole may be refrigerated and baked at a later time.) Bake in preheated 350°F. oven, covered, for about 60 minutes or until rice in center of casserole is cooked, yet firm. Just before serving, sprinkle with chopped parsley.

Yield: 10 servings (1 cup each)
     1 serving = 2 ounces meat
                   ½ teaspoon oil

Tamale Pie

- 1 pound lean ground beef
- 1 medium yellow onion, finely chopped
- 1 10¾-ounce can tomato soup, undiluted
- 1 soup can water
- ½ teaspoon instant beef bouillon granules
- ¼ teaspoon ground black pepper
- ¼ teaspoon salt
- 1 tablespoon chili powder
- 1 cup canned whole kernel corn, drained
- 1 tablespoon yellow corn meal
- ½ cup finely chopped green pepper

Topping:
- ¾ cup yellow corn meal
- 1 tablespoon all-purpose flour
- 1 tablespoon sugar
- ½ teaspoon baking powder
- 1 whole egg
- ⅓ cup skim milk
- 1 tablespoon oil

In a large skillet, brown ground beef; drain on paper towels. Pour off fat from skillet. In same skillet, mix together next nine ingredients and return ground beef to skillet. Simmer, uncovered, 15 minutes. Stir in green pepper. Transfer meat mixture to a 2-quart casserole dish. Prepare cornbread topping by combining dry ingredients, then stirring in liquid ingredients. Cover meat mixture with topping. Bake, uncovered, in a preheated 350°F. oven for 25-35 minutes or until corn bread topping is done.

Yield: 6 servings
     1 serving = 2 ounces meat
                   ½ teaspoon oil
                   ⅙ egg

Lemon Meatballs

- 1½ pounds lean ground beef
- 1 whole egg, slightly beaten
- 1 teaspoon grated lemon rind
- 3 tablespoons lemon juice
- 2 teaspoons salt
- ⅛ teaspoon ground black pepper
- ¼ teaspoon ground thyme
- ¼ teaspoon ground marjoram
- 3 tablespoons finely chopped onion
- ⅓ cup uncooked long grain white rice
- 1 10¾-ounce can tomato soup, undiluted
- 2 cups boiling water

In large bowl, mix together all but the last two ingredients. Shape into approximately 20 balls, each 1½ inches in diameter. Lightly brown meatballs, a few at a time, in a large skillet without added fat. Mix together tomato soup and boiling water; pour over meat. Cover and simmer 30-40 minutes or until rice is cooked but firm. Serve hot.

Yield: 20 meatballs
      1 meatball = 1 ounce meat

Porcupine Meatballs

- ½ cup water
- ½ cup uncooked long grain white rice
- 1 pound lean ground beef
- 1 teaspoon salt
- ⅛ teaspoon ground black pepper
- 1 small yellow onion, sliced into ¼-inch thick rings
- 1 teaspoon margarine
- ½ medium green pepper, cut into ¼-inch thick strips
- 2 cloves garlic, minced
- 1 8-ounce can tomato sauce
- ¼ cup water
- dash ground nutmeg
- ⅛ teaspoon ground black pepper
- ¼ teaspoon salt

In a small saucepan, bring water to a boil; add rice; cover and simmer 5 minutes. Cool and combine with ground beef; add salt and pepper and mix well. Form into eight meatballs. Place in 2-quart baking dish. In a small skillet, brown onion in margarine. Distribute onion and raw green pepper over meatballs. In a small bowl, mix together tomato sauce, water, and spices. Pour mixture over meatballs and vegetables. Cover and bake in a preheated 350°F. oven for 90 minutes or until meat is tender and brown throughout.

Yield: 4 servings
      1 serving = 3 ounces meat

Tasty Burger

- 1 pound lean ground beef
- 1 tablespoon nonfat dry milk powder
- ¼ cup fine dry bread crumbs
- 1 tablespoon margarine
- 1 large yellow onion, cut into ¼-inch slices
- ½ small green pepper, chopped
- 2 English muffins, halved
- 4 teaspoons margarine, divided

Mix ground round with nonfat dry milk powder and bread crumbs. Divide into four patties. Broil patties to desired degree of doneness. Melt margarine in a medium skillet. Sauté onion in margarine until slightly tender. Add green pepper, cook until crisp-tender. Toast English muffins, and spread each half with 1 teaspoon margarine. Place each beef patty on an English muffin half, and top with sautéed vegetables.

Yield: 4 servings
      1 serving = 3 ounces meat
                   1 teaspoon margarine

Curried Kabobs

- 2 pounds lean pork or beef, 1-inch cubes
- 1/3 cup lemon juice
- 1/4 cup oil
- 2 tablespoons shredded onion
- 1 clove garlic, crushed
- 1 tablespoon salt
- 1 teaspoon ground ginger
- 1 1/2 teaspoons curry powder
- 1/4 teaspoon ground red pepper
- 16 fresh mushroom caps
- 1 large green pepper, seeded, cut into 1-inch squares
- 2 tablespoons margarine
- 16 cherry tomatoes
- 4 small white onions, quartered
- 2 8-ounce cans pineapple chunks, packed in own juice

Place meat cubes in a glass dish; cover with marinade made of lemon juice, oil, and seasonings. Refrigerate and marinate for at least 4 hours. When ready to cook kabobs, sauté mushroom caps and green peppers lightly in margarine over medium heat. Remove meat from marinade. Assemble 8 kabobs on 12-inch or longer skewers; alternate meat, vegetables, and pineapple on the skewers. Broil 2-3 inches from heat source or grill over hot coals, 10-15 minutes for both methods. Turn and brush with marinade as necessary. Serve over hot brown rice.

Yield: 8 kabobs
1 kabob = 3 ounces meat

Exquisite Marinated Ham

- 1 cup pineapple juice
- 1 tablespoon oil
- 1/2 teaspoon ground ginger
- 1/3 cup brown sugar
- 2 teaspoons powdered mustard
- 1 tablespoon wine vinegar
- 1 pound (approximately) ham steak, 1-inch thick

In a small bowl, mix together first six ingredients. Marinate ham for at least 12 hours in a flat container. Remove ham from marinade and grill or broil (if broiling, position meat 5 inches from source of heat) for 20-30 minutes. Turn ham, and baste with marinade frequently during broiling.

Yield: 4 servings
1 serving = 3 ounces meat
3/4 teaspoon oil

Sweet and Sour Pork

- 1 1/2 pounds pork tenderloin, trimmed and cut into 1-inch cubes
- 1/4 cup unsifted all-purpose flour
- 1/2 teaspoon salt
- 1/4 teaspoon ground black pepper
- 2 tablespoons oil
- 1 clove garlic, minced
- 1 teaspoon instant chicken bouillon granules
- 1 cup hot water
- 1 5 1/4-ounce can pineapple chunks, packed in own juice, undrained
- 3 large carrots, cut crosswise into 1/4-inch slices
- 2 tablespoons distilled white vinegar
- 2 tablespoons soy sauce
- 1 tablespoon canned mushroom pieces, drained
- 2 tablespoons corn starch
- 1/4 cup cold water
- 1 large green pepper, seeded, cut into large square pieces

Coat meat with flour seasoned with salt and pepper. Using a large skillet, brown meat in oil. Add remaining ingredients to pan except for corn starch, water, and green pepper. Simmer mixture for 45 minutes covered. Mix together corn starch and water. Stir into meat. Add green pepper, and simmer meat mixture with cover on for an additional 15 minutes. Serve over hot rice.

Yield: 5 servings (1 cup each)
1 serving = 3 ounces meat
1 teaspoon oil

Marinated Pork Chops

- 2 tablespoons oil
- ¼ cup plus 2 tablespoons soy sauce
- 2 tablespoons Worcestershire sauce
- 1 tablespoon powdered mustard
- 1 teaspoon salt
- ¼ cup wine vinegar
- 1 teaspoon dried parsley flakes
- ⅓ cup lemon juice
- ½ teaspoon ground black pepper
- 1 clove garlic, crushed
- 6 pork chops, 1-inch thick, fat trimmed (about 3½ pounds total raw weight)

To make marinade, mix together first ten ingredients in a flat-bottom container. Place pork chops in marinade; marinate 4 hours in refrigerator. Remove chops from marinade and broil approximately 5 inches from source of heat for 30 minutes or until done. Turn and baste meat with marinade frequently. Marinade can be refrigerated in a sealable container and used again.

Yield: 6 servings
    1 serving = approximately 5½ ounces meat
    1 teaspoon oil

Quick-Stir Ham and Spinach

- 2 tablespoons finely chopped yellow onion
- 1 clove garlic, minced
- 8 ounces fully cooked ham, cut into match stick-like pieces
- 2 tablespoons oil
- 1 pound fresh spinach, washed and drained (or 2 10-ounce packages frozen spinach, thawed; omit the 2 tablespoons water below)
- 2 tablespoons water
- 2 tablespoons cornstarch
- ¼ cup water

In large skillet, sauté onion, garlic, and ham in oil until lightly browned, stirring frequently. Add spinach and 2 tablespoons water. Cover and continue cooking over medium heat for 5-7 minutes, stirring once or twice. Blend together cornstarch and ¼ cup water. Stir into ham-spinach mixture. Cook at least 1 additional minute, stirring constantly, or until sauce thickens and clears.

Yield: 6 servings (⅔ cup each)
    1 serving = 1 teaspoon oil
    1⅓ ounce meat

Beer-Braised Rabbit

- 1 rabbit, dressed and quartered (approximately 2 pounds)
- salt and pepper
- 2 tablespoons oil
- 3 medium-sized baking (Idaho) potatoes, pared and quartered
- 3-4 large carrots, bias cut 1-inch pieces
- 1 medium yellow onion, cut into ¼-inch thick rings
- 1 cup beer
- ¼ cup chili sauce
- 1 tablespoon brown sugar
- 1 clove garlic, minced
- water
- ⅓ cup cold water
- 3 tablespoons all-purpose flour
- ½ teaspoon salt

Lightly season rabbit to taste with salt and pepper. In a Dutch oven, brown rabbit in hot oil. Add vegetables. In a medium-sized bowl, mix together beer, chili sauce, brown sugar, and garlic. Pour over rabbit and vegetables, cover and simmer 60 minutes. Remove meat and vegetables; keep warm. Strain drippings into measuring cup; skim off fat. Add, if necessary, more water to make 1½ cups liquid; return liquid to Dutch oven. Mix together ⅓ cup cold water, flour, and salt with fork; add slowly to juices in pan. Cook and stir until gravy begins to boil; boil 1 minute, stirring constantly. Return meat and vegetables to Dutch oven; heat well before serving.

Yield: 4 servings
    1 serving = approximately 5 ounces meat
    1½ teaspoons oil

Poultry

Spicy Baked Chicken

- 1 (2½-3 pound) chicken, cut up with excess fat removed
- 2 tablespoons water
- 2 tablespoons flour
- 1 cup evaporated skim milk
- 1 tablespoon instant minced onion
- 1 tablespoon parsley flakes
- 1 teaspoon basil leaves
- ½ teaspoon ground sage
- ½ teaspoon garlic salt
- ¼ teaspoon black pepper

Place chicken on a rack in a shallow roasting pan. Bake in preheated (425°F.) oven for 45 minutes. Meanwhile, mix flour and water until smooth. Blend in evaporated skim milk, and add onion and spices.

Remove chicken from rack. Layer in covered dish. Pour evaporated milk mixture over chicken. Reduce oven to 325°F. Cover and bake 20 minutes or until chicken is tender.

Yield: 6 servings
1 serving = 3-4 ounces meat

Smothered Chicken

- 1 frying chicken, cut into quarters, skin and fat removed
- ½ cup flour
- 1 teaspoon salt
- ¼ teaspoon lemon pepper
- ¾-1 cup chicken broth
- 2 tablespoons margarine, melted paprika

Rinse and dry chicken. Sift flour with salt and lemon pepper. Roll chicken in seasoned flour, placing thick side down in a shallow baking pan. Add broth and melted margarine. Cover and bake at 350°F. for 1 hour and 10 minutes, or until tender. Turn occasionally during the cooking time. Uncover baking dish for part of the time as desired to thicken the broth and brown the chicken. For additional browning, sprinkle with paprika and put under broiler at medium heat. Serve at once.

Chicken bouillon cubes may be used to prepare broth. This broth will become quite thick if the chicken is uncovered for approximately half of the cooking time.

Yield: 4 servings
1 serving = 4 ounces meat
1½ teaspoons margarine

Crunchy Coated Chicken

- 4 tablespoons flour
- ½ cup fine, dry bread crumbs
- ¼ teaspoon dried onion flakes
- ¼ teaspoon garlic powder
- ¼ teaspoon paprika
- ½ teaspoon cornstarch
- ½ teaspoon salt
- ½ teaspoon sugar
- 1 teaspoon margarine
- 1 chicken fryer, cut up (about 3 pounds)
- 2 tablespoons oil

Mix together first eight ingredients. Cut in margarine with a knife or pastry cutter. Skin chicken pieces and brush with 2 tablespoons of oil. Coat with the above mixture and arrange in greased baking dish. Bake at 350°F. for 60 minutes.

Yield: 6 servings
1 serving = approximately 4 ounces meat
approximately 1 teaspoon oil

Sweet and Sour Barbecued Baked Chicken

- 1 cup commercial barbecue sauce
- ⅓ cup apricot preserves
- ¼ cup water
- 1 chicken, cut up (about 3 pounds)

Mix first three ingredients in blender. Remove skin from chicken. Dip chicken in sauce, place in baking pan, and cover with foil. Bake for 60 minutes at 350°F. Remove foil and continue to bake for 30-60 minutes, depending on desired brownness. Baste chicken several times while browning. The amount of sauce needed may vary with the size of the chicken.

Yield: 6 servings
  1 serving = 4 ounces meat

Chicken Fricassee

- 4 pounds frying chicken parts
- 1 medium onion, chopped
- 1 medium carrot, thinly sliced
- 1 stalk celery, thinly sliced
- 2 teaspoons salt
- 6 peppercorns
- 4 whole cloves
- 1 bay leaf
  water
- 3 tablespoons margarine
- 1 teaspoon basil, crumbled
- 6 tablespoons flour
- 1 10-ounce package frozen peas
  Cornmeal Dumplings (below)

Place in a large kettle or Dutch oven: chicken, onion, carrot, celery, salt, peppercorns, cloves, bay leaf, and enough water to cover (about 8 cups). Heat to boiling; cover, lower heat, and simmer 2 hours or until chicken is tender. Remove skin; set chicken aside. Strain stock, remove spices, and save vegetables for use later. Measure stock and either add enough water or condense by boiling to yield 4 cups stock. Cool stock until fat solidifies; skim off fat and discard. In kettle used to cook chicken, melt margarine; add basil and 2 cups of stock. In remaining 2 cups of cold stock, disperse flour by adding slowly and stirring with fork; add to kettle; stir and cook until gravy thickens. Boil 2 minutes. Place chicken in gravy; add vegetables and frozen peas. Heat slowly to simmering while preparing batter for cornmeal dumplings. Drop batter in eight mounds on top of chicken. Cover and steam 20 minutes on low heat until dumplings are puffy-light, arrange chicken and dumplings on platter. Gravy may be passed to spoon over all.

Yield: 8 servings
  1 serving = 4 ounces meat
          1 teaspoon margarine

Cornmeal Dumplings

- 1 cup sifted flour
- 2 teaspoons baking powder
- ½ teaspoon salt
- ¾ cup yellow cornmeal
- 1 cup skim milk
- 2 tablespoons oil

Sift flour, baking powder, and salt together; place in a medium mixing bowl. Add cornmeal; mix well with other dry ingredients. Combine milk and oil. Stir, adding all at once, into flour mixture. Stir just until all liquid is incorporated. Dough will be soft. Cook as directed in recipe for Chicken Fricassee.

Yield: 8 dumplings
  1 dumpling = ¾ teaspoon oil

Chicken Almond

- 2 whole chicken breasts, skinned, boned, and diced (reserve bones)
- 2 cups water
- ½ teaspoon tarragon
- dash thyme
- 1 slice onion
- 1 small carrot
- 1 sprig fresh parsley
- 1 celery top
- ½ teaspoon sugar
- 1 tablespoon white cooking wine
- 1 tablespoon soy sauce
- 1 tablespoon cornstarch mixed with 1 tablespoon water (for marinade)
- 2 tablespoons oil
- ½ cup sliced bamboo shoots
- ½ cup bias-sliced celery
- ½ cup sliced water chestnuts
- ¼ cup shredded onion
- ½ teaspoon salt
- ¼ teaspoon white pepper
- 1 tablespoon cornstarch mixed with 1 tablespoon water (for thickening)
- ½ cup slivered almonds, toasted

To make stock, place breast bones in medium-sized saucepan with water, tarragon, thyme, onion slice, carrot, parsley, and celery top. Simmer covered for 30 minutes. Cool and strain off any fat. Measure 1 cup stock (add water or boil to concentrate stock, if necessary) and reserve for later use.

Combine sugar, wine, soy sauce, and cornstarch-water mixture; marinate diced raw chicken in soy sauce mixture for at least 30 minutes. Stir-fry marinated chicken in 1 tablespoon oil using large, heavy saucepan with tight fitting lid. Cook 3 minutes and steam, covered, for 5 minutes. Remove chicken and place in warm serving casserole dish. Note: Bottom of saucepan should be coated with browned cornstarch.

Add second tablespoon oil to pan. Stir-fry bamboo shoots, celery, water chestnuts, and onion. Cook 4 minutes and steam 5 minutes. Add reserved chicken stock, salt, white pepper, and cornstarch-water mixture. Stir mixture constantly and cook over moderate heat until thickened. Transfer vegetables with sauce to casserole dish containing chicken; stir. Top with toasted almonds and serve.

May be made a day ahead, but do not add nuts until last minute. Reheat in moderate oven at 350°F. for 30 minutes. Undercook vegetables by 1-2 minutes if reheating is planned. Serve with cooked rice.

Yield: 6 servings (½ cup each)
1 serving = 2 ounces meat
1 teaspoon oil

Poulet Dijon

- 2 chickens, quartered and skin removed
- salt and pepper
- ¼ cup margarine
- 2 tablespoons Dijon mustard
- 1 clove garlic, chopped
- ⅓ cup chopped onion
- 1 10½-ounce can condensed chicken broth
- 1 tablespoon flour
- 2 tablespoons finely chopped fresh parsley
- 2 4-ounce cans mushrooms, drained

Sprinkle chicken on all sides with salt and pepper. In large skillet, melt margarine, and brown chicken pieces slowly on all sides. In small bowl, mix remaining ingredients until well blended. Pour mixture over chicken. Simmer, turning pieces occasionally until chicken is tender, about 40 minutes. Arrange chicken pieces on a warm platter, and pour the sauce over all.

Yield: 8 servings
1 serving = 4 ounces meat
1½ teaspoons margarine

French Chicken in Sherry

- 3 whole chicken breasts, split
- ½ teaspoon salt
- 1 medium onion, sliced
- ¼ cup chopped green pepper
- 1 cup sliced mushrooms

Remove excess fat from chicken, keeping skin intact. Place chicken, skin side up, on rack in broiler. Broil 2 inches from heat for 10 minutes until skin is brown. Do not turn. Arrange browned chicken in shallow casserole. Sprinkle with ½ teaspoon of salt. Add onion, green pepper, and mushrooms.

Sauce:
- 1 cup orange juice
- ½ cup dry sherry
- ½ cup water
- 1 tablespoon firmly packed brown sugar
- 1 teaspoon salt
- ¼ teaspoon ground black pepper
- 1 tablespoon flour
- 1 teaspoon grated orange rind
- 2 teaspoons chopped parsley

Combine orange juice, sherry, water, brown sugar, salt, pepper, orange rind, and flour in saucepan. Blend well. Cook on medium heat, stirring constantly until thickened; add parsley. Pour sauce over chicken.

Bake uncovered in 375°F. oven for approximately 45 minutes or until tender. Baste several times while cooking.

Yield: 6 servings (½ breast each)
1 serving = 4 ounces meat

Chicken Thigh Parmigiana

- 4 chicken thighs
- 2 tablespoons margarine
- 1 medium onion, sliced
- ½ teaspoon garlic powder
- 1 package (10 ounces) frozen chopped spinach
- ½ teaspoon salt
- 1 teaspoon dried basil leaves
- ¼ cup grated Parmesan cheese

Skin chicken thighs. Using a large skillet, sauté chicken thighs in melted margarine 5 minutes or until golden brown. Turn occasionally. Add onion and garlic powder; sauté, covered, for 5 minutes. Push chicken to one side of skillet. Add spinach. Sprinkle with salt and basil. Simmer, covered, for 15 minutes. Turn chicken right side up. Sprinkle with ¼ cup grated Parmesan cheese. Blend spinach with onion and margarine. Simmer, covered, for 10 minutes or until the chicken is tender.

Yield: 4 servings
1 serving = 2 ounces meat
1½ teaspoons margarine

Barbecued Chicken Orientale

- 4 whole chicken breasts, halved, skinned, and boned
- 1 cup dry white wine
- 1 can (6 ounces) frozen concentrated apple juice, thawed
- 2 tablespoons soy sauce
- ¼ teaspoon ground ginger
- 2 tablespoons vinegar
- 2 tablespoons oil
- 16 fresh or canned mushrooms
- 2 parboiled whole white onions
- 1 orange, divided into sections
- 16 pineapple chunks
- 16 cherry tomatoes

Cut each half chicken breast into four pieces. Combine wine, apple juice, soy sauce, ginger, vinegar, and oil. Add the chicken, fruit, and vegetables. Marinate in refrigerator at least one hour. Thread each of eight skewers with chicken pieces alternating with fruit and vegetables. Place skewers in shallow pan. Broil about 6 inches from heat for 10 minutes on each side, brushing with marinade every 5 minutes.

Yield: 8 servings
1 serving = 3 ounces of meat
¾ teaspoon oil

Chicken Breasts in Curried Fruit

- 2 tablespoons margarine
- 1 teaspoon curry powder
- 4 half chicken breasts, skinned and boned
- 4 tablespoons dry white wine
- ½ teaspoon salt
- 4 tablespoons raisins
- 1 17-ounce can fruit cocktail, well drained
- 2 tablespoons brown sugar
- ¼ cup sliced almonds

Melt margarine in an 8-inch skillet over medium heat, and stir in curry powder. Add chicken breasts and sauté until golden on both sides. Add wine, salt, and raisins. Cover and simmer slowly over low heat about 5 minutes. To test doneness, press finger into thickest part of chicken breast, meat should spring back. Do not overcook. Place chicken breasts on a plate and cover loosely with skillet lid to keep warm. Quickly add fruit cocktail and brown sugar to pan juices and bring to a boil. Stir and cook until syrupy. Place chicken breasts on plates. Pour sauce over chicken. Garnish with sliced almonds.

Yield: 4 servings
      1 serving = 3 ounces meat
              1½ teaspoons margarine

Breast of Chicken on Rice

- 1 10½-ounce can condensed golden mushroom soup
- 2 soup cans skim milk
- 1 cup white rice, uncooked
- 1 can (4 ounces) mushroom stems and pieces, drained
- ½ envelope (about ¾ ounces) dry onion soup mix
- 2 chicken breasts, split into halves, skin removed

Heat oven to 350°F. Blend mushroom soup and milk. Stir together soup mixture, rice, mushrooms, and the dry onion soup mix. Pour into lightly greased 3-quart baking dish. Arrange chicken breasts in rice mixture. Cover. Bake for 60 minutes. Uncover and bake 15 minutes longer.

Yield: 4 servings
      1 serving = 3 ounces meat

Stuffed Chicken Breasts Olé

- 4 whole chicken breasts, halved, skinned, and boned
- 2 teaspoons instant minced onion
- 2 tablespoons chopped green chilies
- ½ cup grated cheddar cheese
- ¼ cup margarine, melted
- 1 cup saltine cracker crumbs (about 15 crushed crackers)
- ¼ cup grated Parmesan cheese
- 1½ tablespoons taco seasoning mix

Pound each raw chicken piece with mallet to flatten. Blend minced onion and chopped green chilies with cheddar cheese. Divide mixture equally among the flattened chicken pieces, placing a portion toward one end of each piece. Roll up each piece, tucking in ends to completely enclose the filling. Fasten with toothpicks.

Brush each roll with melted margarine to cover. Mix cracker crumbs with grated Parmesan cheese and taco seasoning mix. Roll each coated piece in crumb mixture. Arrange in an 8-inch square baking dish. Cover with foil and bake at 350°F. for 40 minutes. Remove foil and bake 10 minutes longer.

Serving suggestion: Serve on bed of shredded lettuce. Garnish with diced tomatoes and chopped black olives.

Yield: 8 servings
      1 serving = 3 ounces meat
              1½ teaspoons margarine
              approximately ¼ dairy equivalent

Chicken Cataloni

- 2 large chicken breasts, split
- 2 teaspoons Dijon-style mustard
- ½ cup Italian seasoned bread crumbs
- 4 1-ounce slices mozzarella cheese
- 2 tablespoons plus 2 teaspoons margarine
- 2 medium onions, sliced
- ½ pound fresh mushrooms (or a 4-ounce can sliced mushrooms)
- ¼ cup Vermouth or sherry

Remove skin and bone from chicken breasts. Pound each one flat with a meat mallet. Spread the breasts with mustard, and sprinkle each with 1 tablespoon of bread crumbs and place one slice of cheese on top. Roll up, jelly-roll style and secure with a toothpick. Rolls may be seasoned with salt and pepper at this time, if desired.

Brown the rolls in 1 tablespoon of margarine in skillet. When golden brown, about 5 minutes, remove to platter.

In the same skillet, sauté the onions and mushrooms in 1 tablespoon plus 2 teaspoons of margarine until onions are tender. Return chicken breasts to skillet and add Vermouth or sherry. Cover and simmer on low heat for 8-10 minutes until chicken is cooked.

Yield: 4 servings
 1 serving = 3 ounces meat
 2 teaspoons margarine
 ½ dairy equivalent

Chicken Mushroom Cups

- 3 tablespoons margarine
- 1 pound mushrooms, sliced
- 3 tablespoons flour
- 1 13-ounce can evaporated skim milk
- ¼ teaspoon salt
- ⅛ teaspoon ground nutmeg
- 2 cups cooked, diced chicken
- 1 cup frozen peas, uncooked
- ⅛ cup chopped pimiento
- ⅓ cup sherry

Melt margarine in saucepan. Sauté mushrooms lightly. Stir in flour to make paste. Stir in evaporated skim milk, salt, and nutmeg. Simmer for 5 minutes, stirring constantly. Add chicken pieces, frozen peas, pimiento, and sherry. Simmer for 10 minutes, stirring occasionally. Serve in toast cups.

To make toast cups: Spread thin sliced bread with ½ teaspoon allowed margarine on one side. Place each slice of bread in a muffin pan, margarine side down. Bake at 250°F. for 20 minutes. Turn oven to 350°F. and bake for 10 minutes.

Yield: 5 cups, sufficient for 26 toast cups
 1 cup = 2 ounces meat approximately 2 teaspoons margarine

Oriental Chicken Salad

- 2½ cups cooked, cut-up chicken or turkey
- 1 cup chopped celery
- 1 can (8½ ounces) water chestnuts, drained and sliced
- 2 green onions, thinly sliced
- 2 canned pimientos, drained and slivered
- 1 cup bean sprouts, drained
- ⅔ cup mayonnaise-type salad dressing
- 2 tablespoons soy sauce
- 1 tablespoon lemon juice

Toss chicken and vegetables together. Stir mayonnaise-type dressing, soy sauce, and lemon juice together. Toss the two mixtures together and chill.

Yield: 6 servings (1 cup each)
 1 serving = 2 ounces meat approximately 2 teaspoons oil

Poultry Olivini

- 1 cup fresh sliced mushrooms
- ½ cup finely chopped onion
- 4 teaspoons margarine
- 2 tablespoons flour
- 1 13-ounce can evaporated skim milk
- ½ teaspoon salt
- ¼ teaspoon celery salt
- dash ground black pepper
- ½ cup green olives, sliced
- 2 cups cooked, diced turkey or chicken
- 1 cup cooked spaghetti
- 3 tablespoons grated Parmesan cheese
- paprika

In a large skillet, sauté mushrooms and onions in margarine until tender (about 5 minutes). Add flour and toss with sautéed vegetables until well distributed. Add evaporated milk and spices. Cook until thickened and mixture begins to bubble, stirring constantly. Remove from heat and stir in olives, poultry, and spaghetti. Turn into greased 1½-quart casserole and top with cheese. Sprinkle paprika lightly over cheese. Bake at 350°F. for 30 minutes.

Yield: 4 cups
1 serving = 2 ounces meat
1 teaspoon margarine

Curry Sauce for Chicken

- 2 tablespoons margarine
- ⅔ cup peeled and chopped apples
- ⅔ cup chopped onion
- ¼ teaspoon ginger
- 1 teaspoon curry powder
- 1½ tablespoons flour
- ½ teaspoon salt
- 1 cup skim milk
- lemon juice

Melt margarine in saucepan. Stir in apple, onion, ginger, and curry powder. Cook slowly until apple and onion are tender but not brown. Blend in flour and salt. Stir in skim milk, and continue stirring until mixture thickens and comes to a boil. Remove from heat, season to taste with lemon juice.

Note: Serve on baked or broiled chicken or combine with 1-2 cups cooked, diced chicken or turkey and serve over rice.

Yield: 4 servings (½ cup each)
1 serving = 1½ teaspoons margarine

Glazed Cornish Game Hens

- 4 Cornish game hens, thawed
- 1 teaspoon salt
- 2 teaspoons crumbled fresh or dried rosemary
- 1 cup applesauce
- 1 cup white wine
- 1 cup finely chopped dried apricots or pears
- ¼ cup firmly packed brown sugar
- 1 teaspoon grated orange rind
- ¼ teaspoon ground cloves

Remove giblets from thawed game hens. Wipe inside and out with paper towel. Mix salt and crumbled rosemary together, and sprinkle mixture into cavity and over game hens. Roast in preheated 350°F. oven for 60 minutes, turning occasionally for even baking. (Giblets are not used in this recipe.)

In medium saucepan, heat applesauce and wine. Add chopped apricots or pears, brown sugar, orange rind, and cloves. Simmer, covered, for 20 minutes, stirring to blend well. Press mixture through a sieve. Spoon over game hens. Bake 30 minutes longer. Allow to cool 15 minutes before serving.

Yield: 8 servings
1 serving = 4 ounces meat

Fish

Fish Creole (Microwave Oven)

- 1 pound fish fillets (sole, turbot, etc.)
  lemon juice
- 2 tablespoons water
- 2 tablespoons cornstarch
- 1 8-ounce can tomato sauce
- 1 2-ounce can mushrooms, drained
- ½ green pepper, diced
- 1 stalk celery, sliced
- 2 teaspoons instant minced onion
- 1 teaspoon instant chicken bouillon granules
- ⅛ teaspoon thyme
- 8 drops Tabasco sauce

Arrange fillets in a glass dish (12 x 8 x 2 inches) with the thickest pieces to the outside. Combine cornstarch and water in a mixing bowl. Add the remaining ingredients to cornstarch mixture and mix well. Pour evenly over fish. Cover with plastic film pleated and slit to allow for escape of steam. Place in microwave oven and cook on high for 4 minutes, then turn dish half way around and cook for 4 additional minutes. Allow to stand 5 minutes before serving. Microwave wattage for recipe time: 650-700.

Yield: 4 servings
1 serving = 3 ounces meat

Mountain Trout (Microwave Oven)

- 2 fresh 8-ounce trout with skin
- 2 tablespoons lemon juice
- 4 teaspoons margarine, melted
- ¼ cup instant minced onion
- 2 teaspoons slivered almonds
- 2 teaspoons chopped parsley
- ¼ teaspoon paprika
  salt and pepper

Wash fish and pat dry. Combine lemon juice, margarine, onion, almonds, parsley, and paprika. Place equal amounts of this inside each trout. Place fish in a nonmetal container and cover with plastic wrap partially slit down the center. Cook 4 minutes on high in microwave oven or until fish can be flaked with a fork. Do not overcook. Oven wattage for 4 minutes cooking time: 650-700.

Yield: 2 servings
1 serving = 6 ounces meat
2 teaspoons margarine

Highbrow Haddock

- 1 pound frozen haddock
- ¼ cup finely chopped raw onion
- 2 tablespoons margarine
- 2 tablespoons flour
- ¼ teaspoon salt
- ⅛ teaspoon pepper
- 1 cup skim milk
- 4 ounces cheddar cheese, shredded
- 1 8-ounce container of low-fat yogurt
- 1 4-ounce can mushrooms, drained
- 1 cup frozen peas, uncooked
  paprika

In large skillet, barely cover haddock with water. Simmer gently 12-15 minutes or until fish flakes with a fork; drain. Break fish into chunks, set aside. In a saucepan, cook onion in the margarine until tender but not brown. Blend in flour, salt, and pepper. Stir in skim milk gradually. Cook over medium heat, stirring constantly until mixture thickens and bubbles. Remove from heat, add cheese and stir until melted. Combine cheese sauce, yogurt, fish, mushrooms, and peas. Bake at 400°F. for 15-20 minutes. Garnish with paprika. Serve over rice.

Yield: 4 servings
1 serving = 3 ounces meat
1½ teaspoons margarine
1 ounce cheese

Curried Catfish

- 2 pounds catfish fillets
- 4 tablespoons margarine
- 1 medium onion, sliced
- 1 tablespoon flour
- 1 teaspoon curry powder
- 2½ cups water
- 1 6-ounce can tomato paste
- 1 teaspoon salt
- ½ teaspoon pepper
- ¼ teaspoon cayenne pepper
- 1 tablespoon lemon juice

Cut catfish into pieces about 1½ inch square. Melt the margarine in a saucepan; fry the fish slightly, then remove fish and set aside. Add the sliced onion, flour, curry powder, and 1 cup water to the margarine and simmer until the onions are tender. Stir constantly. Stir in tomato paste and 1½ cups water. Add remaining spices and simmer for 10 minutes. Bring nearly to boiling point then add fish and lemon juice. Cover and heat gently for 10-15 minutes. Stir occasionally to prevent fish from sticking to bottom of saucepan. Serve over rice.

Yield: 6 servings
  1 serving = 4 ounces meat
  2 teaspoons margarine

Mediterranean Baked Fish

- 1 tablespoon oil
- 1 large onion, diced
- 3 large fresh tomatoes, chopped (or a 1-pound can, well drained)
- 1 clove garlic, minced
- 1 cup white wine
- 1 cup clam juice
- 1 bay leaf
- ½ teaspoon dried oregano
- ¼ teaspoon dried thyme
- ¼ teaspoon dried basil
- 1 tablespoon grated orange peel
  freshly ground pepper
  salt to taste
- 1 teaspoon fennel seeds, crushed
- 1 pound fish fillets (sole, flounder, sea perch, etc.)

Sauté onion in oil until soft. Add remaining ingredients except fish; stir well and simmer for about one-half hour, uncovered, until a good flavor develops. Arrange fish in a shallow bake-serve dish and pour sauce over fish. Bake at 350°F. about 15 minutes until fish is done. Serve at once.

Yield: 4 servings
  1 serving = 3 ounces meat
  ¾ teaspoon oil

Fish Fillets in a Package

- 2 fish fillets (about 1 pound)
- 1 tablespoon margarine
- 1 tablespoon lemon juice

Either of the following seasoning combinations:

- ¼ teaspoon salt
- ½ teaspoon dill weed
- ⅛ teaspoon black pepper
  dash MSG

OR

- ¼ teaspoon salt
- ¼ teaspoon rosemary leaves, crushed
- ⅛ teaspoon tarragon
- ⅛ teaspoon fennel seed, crushed
  dash black pepper

Place fillets on a piece of heavy-duty aluminum foil. Thoroughly blend together one of the seasoning combinations given and the margarine and lemon juice. Spread over top of fillets. Fold aluminum foil to make a package. Seal edges. Place package on grill about 5 inches from coals. (Package may also be placed in the oven at about 350°F. for about 30 minutes.) Cook 20 minutes or until fish can be flaked easily with a fork. Turn package over after 10 minutes cooking time.

Yield: 4 servings
  1 serving = 3 ounces meat
  ¾ teaspoon margarine

Oven-Fried Fish

- 2 pounds fish fillets
- 1 cup white cooking wine
- 1 cup seasoned bread crumbs
- 2 tablespoons plus 2 teaspoons margarine
- 1 teaspoon parsley flakes
- fresh lemon

Spray a baking sheet with nonstick cooking spray. Dip fillets in ½ cup of wine, then in bread crumbs, turning to coat both sides. Place pieces on baking sheet. Sprinkle fillets lightly with remaining ½ cup of wine, allowing wine to drip onto the baking sheet around the fish. Melt margarine and stir in parsley. Spoon margarine down the center of fillets. Bake at 450°F. for approximately 15 minutes or until fish flakes easily. Serve garnished with lemon quarters.

Yield: 8 servings
    1 serving = 3 ounces meat
                      1 teaspoon margarine

Sautéed Fish with Oranges

- 4 oranges
- 1 pound fish fillets (red snapper, sea bass, turbot, etc.)
- 4 teaspoons margarine
- 4 teaspoons lemon juice
- 1 clove garlic, crushed
- salt and pepper

Cut unpeeled oranges into thin slices, then cut each in half. Store in refrigerator until needed.

In a pan, melt margarine; add lemon juice and garlic. Place fillets in lemon-margarine mixture. Sauté on both sides, basting top with the lemon-margarine mixture. Fish is done when it flakes easily; do not overcook. Salt and pepper to taste. Place each fillet in individual serving dishes and surround with orange slices.

Yield: 4 servings
    1 serving = 3 ounces meat
                      1 teaspoon margarine

Herbed Fish Sauterne

- 1 pound fish fillets (bass, halibut, salmon, trout, etc.)
- ½ cup Sauterne or white cooking wine
- 4 teaspoons margarine
- ¼ cup lemon juice
- 1 clove garlic
- pinch of leaf rosemary
- ¼ teaspoon parsley flakes
- ¼ teaspoon dried chives

Marinate fish in wine one-half hour, then drain. In small saucepan, melt margarine. Add lemon juice, garlic, rosemary, parsley, and chives. Use frequently to baste fish while broiling. Broil for 20 minutes or until fish flakes easily.

Yield: 4 servings
    1 serving = 3 ounces meat
                      1 teaspoon margarine

Greek Fish and Vegetables

- 1 whole white fish (about 3 pounds)
- 2 tablespoons oil
- 1½ cups chopped onion
- 2 cloves garlic, minced
- 1½ cups drained canned tomatoes
- ½ cup snipped fresh parsley
- ¼ cup snipped fresh dill or 1 tablespoon dried dill
- ½ teaspoon salt
- ¼ teaspoon pepper
- 2 tablespoons lemon juice
- 1 pound raw spinach
- ½ cup dry white wine

Sauté onions in oil until soft. Add garlic, tomatoes, parsley, dill, salt, and pepper. Cook 10 minutes. Sprinkle fish with lemon juice. Arrange tomato mixture in 13 x 9 x 2-inch pan. Lay fish on top, arrange spinach around it. Pour wine over it; cover with foil. Bake 30 minutes at 350°F. Uncover and bake 15 minutes longer.

Yield: 6 servings
    1 serving = 6 ounces meat
                      1 teaspoon oil

Flounder Marinara

- 1 cup sliced onion
- 2 tablespoons margarine
- 2 tablespoons cornstarch
- 1 16-ounce can stewed tomatoes, well drained
- ½ teaspoon dried basil leaves
- 1 pound frozen flounder fillets
- ¼ cup grated Parmesan cheese

Sauté onion in margarine for approximately 5 minutes. Remove onions and set aside. Stir in cornstarch. Then, add tomatoes and basil. Mix well and transfer tomato mixture to baking dish. Place onions on top of tomato mixture. Slice frozen fillets into six pieces (thaw slightly if necessary). Sprinkle with Parmesan. Bake covered 15-20 minutes at 375°F. Remove cover and broil 5-7 minutes or until cheese is golden brown.

Yield: 6 servings
    1 serving = 2 ounces meat
             1 teaspoon margarine

Tomato Crown Fish

- 1 pound fish fillets
  salt and pepper
- 1 cup fresh tomato wedges
- ½ medium green pepper, chopped
- 2 tablespoons chopped onion
- ½ cup Italian seasoned bread crumbs
- 1 tablespoon plus 1 teaspoon margarine, melted
- ½ teaspoon basil

After freshening fish (see *Cooking Terms*), place on a greased baking sheet. Season lightly with salt and pepper. Spread tomato wedges over fillets. Sprinkle with green pepper and onion. Combine seasoned bread crumbs, margarine, and basil. Sprinkle this mixture evenly over vegetables. Bake at 350°F. for approximately 15 minutes or until fish flakes easily.

Yield: 4 servings
    1 serving = 3 ounces meat
             1 teaspoon margarine

Scallop Paella

- 1 cup rice, uncooked
- ¼ teaspoon ground thyme
- 2 teaspoons dried parsley
- 2 tablespoons margarine
- ½ teaspoon salt
- ¼ teaspoon basil
- 1 medium green pepper, cut in strips
- 1 medium red pepper, cut in strips
- 1 pound scallops

Freshen scallops (see *Cooking Terms*), pat dry, and set aside. Prepare desired type of rice according to package directions. Add thyme and parsley to rice at the start of cooking. Ten minutes before rice is scheduled to be done, slice peppers. Melt margarine in large frying pan over low heat. Add salt, basil, peppers, and scallops. Cook over medium heat for 3 minutes while stirring. Add cooked rice to scallop mixture; toss.

Yield: 6 servings
    1 serving = 2 ounces meat
             1 teaspoon margarine

Golden Fish Puffs

- 4 4-ounce fish fillets
  salt and pepper
- 1 egg white
- ⅛ teaspoon salt
- ¼ cup mayonnaise-type salad dressing
- ¼ teaspoon dill seed
- ¼ teaspoon onion juice
  paprika

Heat oven to 425°F. Place fillets in greased baking dish. Season lightly with salt and pepper. Beat egg white and salt until stiff but not dry. Fold in remaining ingredients. Cover fillets with topping. Bake, uncovered, approximately 20 minutes or until topping is brown and puffed. Sprinkle top with paprika.

Yield: 4 servings
    1 serving = 3 ounces meat
             1 teaspoon oil

Mexican Fish Steaks

- 4 small halibut or cod steaks (3 pounds total weight)
- 2 tablespoons oil
- 1 cup chopped onions
- ¼ pound fresh button mushrooms (optional)
- ½ cup chopped green pepper
- 1 small clove garlic, minced
- 1 16-ounce can whole tomatoes, drained
- 1 teaspoon salt
- ¼ teaspoon pepper
- ⅛ teaspoon thyme
- ⅛ teaspoon basil
- ⅛ teaspoon cayenne pepper

Thoroughly dry fish steaks with paper towel. Heat oil in large deep skillet over medium heat. Add fish and brown lightly, turning once (2-3 minutes). Arrange fish in baking dish. Sauté onions, mushrooms, green pepper, and garlic in skillet until tender. Stir in tomatoes, salt, and spices and cook 1 minute. Pour tomato mixture over fish. Bake at 400°F. about 20 minutes or until fish flakes easily.

Yield: 6 servings
    1 serving = 6 ounces meat
               1 teaspoon oil

Tarragon-Sautéed Scallops

- 2 tablespoons plus 2 teaspoons margarine
- ½ teaspoon tarragon
- 2 cups sliced fresh mushrooms
- 3 tablespoons chopped green onions
- 1 pound fresh scallops, washed and dried
- 1 tablespoon dry white wine

Melt margarine in large frying pan over medium high heat; stir in tarragon. Add the mushrooms and green onions, and sauté until just tender. Push the vegetables to the side of the pan, and add the scallops. Sauté on both sides a total of about 4 minutes. Sprinkle with the wine, and cook 1 minute longer. Gently mix the scallops with the mushrooms and green onions. Garnish with chopped parsley and a wedge of lemon if desired.

Yield: 4 servings
    1 serving = 3 ounces meat
              2 teaspoons margarine

Crab Cakes

- 2 6-ounce cans crab meat, undrained
- 2 egg whites
- ¼ cup plus 2 tablespoons mayonnaise-type salad dressing
- 1 teaspoon Worcestershire sauce
- 1 cup fine, dry bread crumbs
- ½ teaspoon salt
- ¼ teaspoon pepper
- 1 teaspoon dried parsley
- 2 teaspoons paprika
- ⅛ teaspoon celery salt
- ½ teaspoon dry mustard

Place crab meat in a mixing bowl with liquid from can. Separate pieces. In a small mixing bowl, combine egg whites, salad dressing, and Worcestershire sauce. Add this mixture to the crab meat, and stir until pieces are coated with sauce. In a separate bowl, combine bread crumbs and spices. Add crumb-spice mixture to the crab meat in small quantities, stirring after each addition until crumbs are moistened. Form crab meat mixture into six cakes approximately 2½ inches in diameter. Preheat oven and broil for approximately 7 minutes or until cakes are browned.

Yield: 6 servings
    1 serving = 2 ounces meat
              1½ teaspoons oil

Salmon Loaf with Almondine Sauce

Salmon Loaf:
- 1 16-ounce can salmon, deboned and cleaned, with liquid
- 2/3 cup evaporated skim milk*
- 2 cups soft bread pieces
- 1 egg
- 1 tablespoon dry parsley
- 2 tablespoons chopped onion
- 1/2 teaspoon salt
- 1/4 teaspoon poultry seasoning

Place salmon in bowl with liquid from can. Flake salmon slightly. Add milk and bread pieces. Blend with fork until only small chunks of salmon are visible. Do not overmix. Add egg and remaining ingredients. Mix. Turn salmon mixture into a greased 8½ x 4½ x 2-inch loaf pan. Bake at 375°F. for approximately 40 minutes or until center is firm. Serve with almondine sauce.

*If a 13-ounce can is purchased, the remainder is sufficient for preparing the sauce recipe.

Almondine Sauce:
- 2 tablespoons margarine
- 3 tablespoons flour
- 1/4 teaspoon salt
- evaporated skim milk remaining from salmon loaf (approximately 1 cup)
- 2 tablespoons skim milk
- 1/4 cup chopped almonds
- 1/4 cup ripe olives, chopped
- 2 tablespoons mayonnaise-type salad dressing
- 1/4 teaspoon lemon juice

Melt margarine in saucepan over low heat. Blend in flour and salt. In separate pan, combine evaporated skim milk and skim milk and scald. While stirring rapidly, add hot milk to flour mixture all at once. Continue to cook and stir until sauce thickens and bubbles. Remove from heat and add almonds, olives, and salad dressing. Cool sauce slightly and stir in lemon juice.

Yield: 6 servings
1 serving = 2 ounces meat
1 teaspoon margarine
1/2 teaspoon oil

Tuna Imperial

- 2 7-ounce cans water-packed tuna
- 1 cup skim milk
- 4 tablespoons all-purpose flour
- 2 tablespoons margarine
- 1/2 teaspoon dry mustard
- 1/2 teaspoon salt
- 1/4 teaspoon white pepper
- 1 teaspoon Worcestershire sauce
- 1/2 teaspoon dill seed
- 1 tablespoon chopped parsley
- 6 tablespoons mayonnaise-type salad dressing

Make a light white sauce by putting milk and flour in a shaker and shaking vigorously to mix. Melt margarine in small saucepan, stir in blended milk and flour. Stirring constantly, cook over medium heat until thickened and bubbling. Stir in seasonings and 2 tablespoons salad dressing. Remove from heat. Pour over drained tuna and mix lightly.

Turn mixture into 4 ramekins or a 1-quart casserole. Spread remaining salad dressing on top in a thin layer. Bake in 375°F. oven for 20 minutes or until lightly browned. Serve hot.

Yield: 4 servings 2/3 cup each
1 serving = 3½ ounces meat
2 teaspoons oil

Pasta & Grains

Pizza

Basic Pizza Dough:
- 1 package dry (granular) yeast
- 1 tablespoon margarine
- 1 teaspoon salt
- 3 cups flour

Topping:
- 1½ teaspoons sugar
- 1 12-ounce can tomato paste
- 10 ounces tomato sauce
- 2 teaspoons garlic salt
- 1½ teaspoons oregano
- 12 ounces mozzarella cheese, grated

Disperse yeast in ¼ cup lukewarm water. Melt margarine in 1 cup of warm water. Combine yeast and margarine mixtures. Add salt and flour gradually. When dough is stiff, flour hands and knead for 10 minutes or until smooth and elastic. Add more flour if needed. Place in greased bowl, cover with a cloth, and set in a warm place for 1½ hours. Punch down and knead lightly. Pat and stretch dough to fit three greased 12-inch pans. Pinch edges up. Let rise 15 minutes.

Oil top of dough. Mix first five topping ingredients and spread on prepared dough. Sprinkle with cheese. Bake in preheated 400°F. oven for 20 minutes or until golden.

Yield: 3 12-inch pizzas
1 pizza = 2 dairy equivalents
1 teaspoon margarine

Linguini with Clam Sauce

- ½ pound linguini
- 3 cloves garlic, peeled
- ¼ cup margarine
- 2 6½-ounce cans minced clams, undrained
- ¼ cup chopped parsley
- ¼ teaspoon basil or thyme leaves

Prepare linguini according to package directions. Meanwhile, in a saucepan, sauté garlic in margarine until lightly browned. Discard garlic. Add clams; heat. Add parsley and seasonings. Heat through and toss with linguini.

Yield: 6 servings (1 cup each)
1 serving = 2 ounces meat
2 teaspoons margarine

Fettucini and Broccoli

- 1 8-ounce package fettucini
- 1 tablespoon margarine
- 1 tablespoon oil
- 1 clove garlic, crushed
- 1 10-ounce package frozen broccoli cuts, thawed and drained
- ⅓ cup canned condensed chicken broth
- ½ teaspoon crushed dried basil leaves
- ⅓ cup chopped fresh parsley
- ¼ cup grated Parmesan cheese
- 1½ cups low-fat (2%) cottage cheese
- ½ teaspoon salt
- dash pepper
- 1 tablespoon grated Parmesan cheese

Prepare fettucini according to package directions. Drain and add 1 tablespoon margarine, toss gently. In uncovered, medium-sized skillet, place 1 tablespoon oil; sauté garlic, broccoli, and oil over medium heat for 5 minutes. Add chicken broth, basil, parsley, Parmesan and cottage cheese, salt and pepper. Stir over low heat until cottage cheese begins to melt. Pour off all but ¼ cup liquid from broccoli mixture. Toss broccoli with fettucini. Transfer to a heated serving dish. Top with 1 tablespoon Parmesan cheese.

Yield: 6 servings (1 cup each)
1 serving = ½ teaspoon margarine
½ teaspoon oil

Rice Dressing

- 2½ cups water
- 1 teaspoon salt
- 1 teaspoon instant chicken bouillon granules or 1 bouillon cube
- 1⅓ cups uncooked long grain white rice
- 2 tablespoons margarine
- 2 tablespoons finely chopped onion
- 1 cup finely chopped celery
- 2 tablespoons finely chopped green pepper
- 1 cup canned mushroom pieces, drained
- ½ cup canned water chestnuts, sliced and drained
- ½ cup chopped pecans
- ¼ teaspoon ground nutmeg
- ¼ teaspoon ground sage
- ¼ teaspoon ground black pepper

In medium-sized saucepan, bring water to a boil. Add salt, chicken bouillon, and rice; stir. Cover and simmer for 20 minutes. Remove from heat; let stand 5 minutes or until all water is absorbed. In a large skillet, melt margarine; sauté onions and celery in margarine over medium heat for 3 minutes. Add green pepper and mushrooms; sauté 2 additional minutes. Add water chestnuts, pecans, and spices; stir. Combine rice with vegetables; toss. Transfer to a heated serving dish.

Yield: 12 servings (½ cup each)
1 serving = ½ teaspoon margarine

Rice with Orange

- ½ teaspoon salt
- 1¼ cups water
- 1½ cups instant rice
- ¼ white onion, finely chopped
- 1 cup finely chopped celery
- 2 tablespoons margarine
- 2 tablespoons concentrated frozen orange juice, unreconstituted

In a medium saucepan, bring salted water to a boil; add rice. Once boiling has begun again, cover and remove pot from heat and set aside. Using a large, heavy skillet, sauté onion and celery in margarine 10-15 minutes over low to medium heat until onion is transparent, but not yellow. To skillet, add concentrated orange juice and rice; stir. Transfer to a heated serving dish. Serve hot with grilled chicken or other fowl.

Yield: 6 servings (½ cup each)
1 serving = 1 teaspoon margarine

Chinese Fried Rice

- 1½ teaspoons oil
- 2 whole eggs, well beaten
- 1 tablespoon oil
- 2 green onions, cut into ½-inch pieces, green and white parts separated
- 3 cups cooked long grain rice
- 1 tablespoon soy sauce
- ¼ cup cooked, finely chopped lean meat or poultry
- ½ cup frozen chopped carrots and peas, half-cooked
- 1 8-ounce can water chestnuts, drained, sliced ⅛ inch thick (optional)

In large, heavy frying pan or wok, place 1½ teaspoons oil; slowly cook beaten egg over very low heat without scrambling. When firm in center, remove; cool and cut 2 x ¼-inch strips and set aside. Add 1 tablespoon oil to pan. Over high heat, stir-fry white part of green onions 3 minutes, then add green parts; sauté until white parts are tender. Add rice, soy sauce, meat, and vegetables. Mix well. Add egg strips and mix gently. Transfer to a heated serving dish.

Yield: 4 servings (1 cup each)
1 serving = 1 teaspoon oil
½ egg
¼ ounce meat

Rice Turmeric

- ¼ cup coarsely chopped onion
- 2 tablespoons water
- 1 tablespoon margarine
- 1 cup long grain white rice, uncooked
- 2 cups boiling water
- 2 teaspoons instant chicken bouillon granules (or 2 bouillon cubes)
- 1 teaspoon salt
- ½ teaspoon ground turmeric
- 1 bay leaf

In large saucepan, cook onion in water and margarine over medium heat for 2-3 minutes or until tender. Add rice and stir to coat grains of rice with margarine. Add water, chicken bouillon, salt, turmeric, and bay leaf. Transfer to a lightly oiled 1-quart casserole; cover tightly and bake in a preheated 375°F. oven for 40-50 minutes or until rice is desirably tender and dry. Add additional stock, if necessary. Remove bay leaf before serving.

Yield: 6 servings (½ cup each)
1 serving = ½ teaspoon margarine

Bread Stuffing

- 1 cup finely chopped onion
- 1½ cups diced celery
- 2 tablespoons margarine
- 1 chicken bouillon cube
- ¾ cup boiling water
- 8 cups dry, coarse bread crumbs
- 1 teaspoon poultry seasoning
- 1 teaspoon ground sage
- ½ teaspoon salt
- ¼ teaspoon ground black pepper
- ¼ teaspoon powdered mustard (optional)
- ¼ cup hottest tap water

Sauté onions and celery in margarine, stirring continuously, for 5 minutes or until desirably tender. Dissolve bouillon cube in boiling water; set aside. Gently toss bread with celery and onions, mix in seasonings. Add bouillon and toss lightly. Turn into a lightly oiled 9 x 5 x 3-inch loaf pan and cover tightly with aluminum foil. Bake in a preheated 300°F. oven for 30 minutes. Add hot tap water; recover and continue baking for 30 minutes more.

Yield: 7 servings (½ cup each)
1 serving = ½ teaspoon margarine

Granola Crunch

- ½ cup oil
- ½ cup honey
- ½ cup crunchy peanut butter
- ⅓ cup firmly packed brown sugar
- 4½ cups old-fashioned rolled oats, uncooked
- 1 cup raw wheat germ
- ½ cup instant nonfat dry milk powder
- 1 cup finely diced or chopped dried fruit (apples, apricots, dates, figs, prunes, raisins, etc.)

In an uncovered small saucepan, combine oil, honey, peanut butter, and brown sugar. Heat until mixture begins to simmer; remove from heat and cool slightly. Mix together remaining ingredients except dried fruit in a 13 x 9 x 2-inch baking pan. Pour heated peanut butter mixture over dry ingredients; mix well. Bake in a preheated 325°F. oven for 20-25 minutes. Stir frequently to toast evenly. Remove from oven; add dried fruit. Cool thoroughly; store at room temperature in airtight container or plastic bag.

Yield: 18 servings (½ cup each)
1 serving = 1⅓ teaspoons oil

Vegetables

Champignons Sautés à la Bordelaise
(Mushrooms Sautéed with Shallots, Garlic, and Herbs)

To Garnish a Meat or Vegetable Platter

- ½ pound fresh mushrooms, whole if small, quartered if large
- 4 teaspoons margarine
- 3 tablespoons finely chopped shallots or green onions
- 1 small clove garlic, minced (optional)
- 3 tablespoons fine, dry, white bread crumbs
- 3 tablespoons fresh parsley, minced
- salt and pepper to taste

Sauté mushrooms in margarine until lightly browned. Stir in shallots or green onions, garlic, and bread crumbs, and toss over moderate heat for 2-3 minutes. Just before serving, season to taste with salt and pepper and toss with parsley.

Yield: 4 servings (½ cup each)
    1 serving = 1 teaspoon margarine

Savory Fried Peppers

- 4 large green peppers, washed and seeded
- 2 tablespoons margarine
- 2 tablespoons oil
- 1 clove garlic, minced
- 1 teaspoon salt
- ⅛ teaspoon pepper
- 1 teaspoon oregano leaves

Cut peppers in 1½-inch wide strips. Heat oil and margarine in a wide frying pan over medium heat. Add pepper strips and minced garlic. Cook, stirring occasionally, until lightly browned. Season with salt, pepper, and oregano. Cover and cook over low heat for 15 minutes or until tender. Serve as an accompaniment to meats.

Yield: 4 servings
    1 serving = 1½ teaspoons margarine
                   1½ teaspoons oil

Oriental Asparagus

- 1 10-ounce package frozen, or 20 fresh, asparagus spears
- 4-5 tablespoons dry sherry, divided
- 1 teaspoon cornstarch
- 1 tablespoon cold water
- 1 tablespoon soy sauce
- 1 tablespoon margarine

Prepare fresh or frozen asparagus, cooking stalks in a skillet with enough water to cover the bottom of the pan. Add 1-2 tablespoons dry sherry to the cooking water for added flavor. Cook until just tender.

Mix cornstarch with cold water. Add this mixture along with soy sauce, 3 tablespoons sherry, and margarine to a small saucepan. Cook for a few minutes over medium heat, adding a little more water if necessary to make a thin sauce. Drain cooked asparagus. Put into serving dish and pour sauce over. Serve with rice.

Yield: 4 servings
    1 serving = ¾ teaspoon margarine

Eggplant Parmesan

Sauce:
- 3 8-ounce cans tomato sauce
- ½ teaspoon garlic powder or a large clove garlic, minced
- ½ teaspoon dried basil
- ½ teaspoon oregano
- ¾ teaspoon fennel seed

In small saucepan, combine all ingredients. Bring to boil and simmer for 20 minutes, stirring occasionally. Prepare the eggplant.

Eggplant:
- 1 medium eggplant, unpeeled and cut in ½-inch slices
- 1 cup skim milk
- ½ cup unsifted flour
- 2 eggs, well beaten
- 2 tablespoons water
- 1 tablespoon minced fresh parsley
- 1 tablespoon chopped green onion
- 1 cup fine, dry bread crumbs
- 4 ounces grated Parmesan cheese (about ½ cup)
- 1 cup shredded mozzarella cheese

Marinate the eggplant slices in the milk for 15 minutes. Remove eggplant and discard milk. Place the flour in one bowl; combine eggs, water, parsley, and green onion in another bowl; and the bread crumbs in a third bowl. Dip each eggplant slice in the flour, then egg mixture, then bread crumbs, coating well. Layer the slices in a lightly oiled 9 x 13-inch pan (slices may overlap but should not cover each other). Cover each layer with sauce and sprinkle with Parmesan cheese. Cover and bake at 350°F. for 30-35 minutes or until slices are tender and easily pierced with a fork. Top with mozzarella cheese and return, uncovered, to oven just until cheese melts.

Yield: 8 servings
1 serving = 1 dairy equivalent

Ratatouille (Zucchini and Eggplant)

- 1 medium eggplant (about 1½ pounds)
- 2 small zucchini (about ½ pound total)
- 1 cup finely chopped green pepper
- ½ cup finely chopped onion
- 4 medium tomatoes, peeled and quartered
- 1 clove garlic, crushed
- 2 teaspoons salt
- ¼ teaspoon ground black pepper
- 3 tablespoons oil

Cut unpared eggplant and zucchini into ½-inch cubes. In a large skillet with cover, cook and stir all ingredients together in oil until heated through. Cover; cook over medium heat, stirring occasionally, about 10 minutes or until vegetables are tender.

Yield: 8 servings (¾ cup each)
1 serving = 1 teaspoon oil

Stuffed Acorn Squash

- 2 acorn squash
- 1 cup applesauce
- 2 teaspoons brown sugar
- 4 teaspoons dry sherry (optional)
- 4 teaspoons margarine

Preheat oven to 400°F. Cut each squash in half lengthwise. Place halves, cut side down, in a shallow baking pan. Cover bottom of pan with water, and bake for 50-60 minutes or until tender. Turn squash over. Mix remaining ingredients, except margarine, together and fill each cavity with the mixture. Dot each half with 1 teaspoon margarine, and continue baking at 400°F. for 15-20 minutes.

Yield: 4 servings
1 serving = 1 teaspoon margarine

Potato Pancakes

- *3 cups peeled, finely shredded raw potatoes
- *1 tablespoon white vinegar or lemon juice
- 1 tablespoon onion, grated
- 2 eggs
- 2 tablespoons whole wheat flour
- 1 teaspoon salt
- pepper to taste
- ½ teaspoon baking powder
- 3 tablespoons plus 1 teaspoon oil

Combine shredded potatoes with onion and eggs until well mixed. Mix onion and eggs into potatoes. Mix together flour, salt, pepper, and baking powder. Blend into potato mixture. Place 1 tablespoon oil in heavy frying pan or electric frying pan and heat until oil is very hot. (A few drops of water should dance around the skillet.)

Using ⅓ cup batter for each pancake, drop potato mixture into hot oil. Brown on both sides over moderately high heat, turning only once. (Can fry several at a time.) One tablespoon oil should fry three pancakes. Serve pancakes crisp and hot.

*After first potato is shredded, toss with vinegar or lemon juice. Stir in remaining potatoes immediately after grating to prevent discoloration.

Yield: 10 pancakes (10 servings)
1 serving = 1 teaspoon oil

Potato Latkes

- 1½ cups peeled and shredded raw red potatoes
- ⅓ cup peeled and grated white onion
- 2 whole eggs, well beaten
- ½ cup unsifted all-purpose flour
- 1 teaspoon salt

Squeeze as much liquid as possible from potatoes; discard liquid. In large mixing bowl, combine all ingredients. Stir to make a smooth batter. By hand, mold batter into 4-inch pancakes. Place on lightly oiled cookie sheet and bake in a preheated 350°F. oven for 20-25 minutes. Serve browned side up.

Yield: 12 potato pancakes

Oven-Fried Potatoes

- 8 large unpeeled baking potatoes, each cut into 8 wedges lengthwise
- ¼ cup oil
- 2 tablespoons grated Parmesan cheese
- ½ teaspoon garlic powder
- ½ teaspoon paprika
- ¼ teaspoon ground black pepper

Arrange potato wedges, peel side down, on two cookie sheets. Mix remaining ingredients together well and brush over potatoes. Bake in preheated 375°F. oven 45 minutes or until potatoes are golden brown and tender. Brush occasionally with oil mixture.

Yield: 8 servings (8 wedges each)
1 serving = 1½ teaspoons oil

Corn Casserole

- 1 16-ounce can whole kernel corn
- 2 eggs
- 2 tablespoons flour
- 2 tablespoons sugar
- 2 tablespoons margarine, melted
- ½ cup grated cheddar cheese

Combine corn, eggs, flour, sugar, margarine, and ¼ cup of cheese in a 1½-quart casserole. Cover and bake at 375°F. for 40 minutes; then sprinkle on remaining ¾ cup cheese, and bake uncovered at 350°F. for 15 minutes.

Yield: 6 servings (½ cup each)
1 serving = 1 teaspoon margarine
⅔ dairy equivalent
⅓ egg

Pineapple-Baked Parsnips

1½ pounds parsnips (about 6 medium)
½ cup pineapple juice
1 teaspoon sugar
1 teaspoon salt
  pepper
1 tablespoon margarine

Cut each parsnip into quarters lengthwise and place in boiling water (enough to cover); cook until tender. Place parsnips in ungreased baking dish. Mix juice, sugar, and salt together; pour over parsnips. Sprinkle with pepper to taste and dot with margarine. Cover, bake 40-45 minutes at 350°F.

Yield: 6 servings
1 serving = ½ teaspoon margarine

Orange Beets

2 tablespoons cornstarch
¾ cup water
1 6-ounce can frozen orange juice concentrate, thawed
¾ cup vinegar
1¼ cups firmly packed brown sugar
1 tablespoon margarine
1 29-ounce can sliced beets, drained (about 3½ cups)

Make a paste of cornstarch and water. Set aside. Mix in saucepan: orange juice, vinegar, and brown sugar; bring to boil. Add cornstarch paste. Stir and cook until thick. Add margarine, then beets. Heat well.

Yield: 8 servings (½ cup each)
1 serving = ½ teaspoon margarine

Green Beans Lyonnaise

1 pound fresh green beans, cut in ½-inch slices
2 medium onions, thinly sliced
2 tablespoons oil
1 teaspoon salt
¼ teaspoon ground black pepper
1 tablespoon chopped fresh parsley
1 tablespoon lemon juice

Place beans in boiling water (enough to cover) and cook until tender. Drain. In skillet, sauté onions in hot oil until lightly browned. Add green beans, salt, and pepper. Sprinkle with parsley and lemon juice.

Yield: 6 servings (¾ cup each)
1 serving = 1 teaspoon oil

Black Beans

1 pound dried black beans
7 cups water
1 teaspoon garlic powder
1 green pepper, chopped
1 onion, chopped
2 tablespoons oil
2 bay leaves
  salt to taste
1 tablespoon vinegar (or lemon juice)
1 small jar pimiento, sliced

Soak beans overnight. Drain beans and place in large covered pot with 7 cups water and remaining ingredients except vinegar or lemon juice. Bring to boil, reduce heat, and simmer about 4-5 hours or until beans are thickened and creamy. Stir and mash beans while simmering to make them creamy. When ready to serve, remove bay leaves and add vinegar or lemon juice. Garnish with pimiento. Wedges of lemon may be served on side. Serve with rice.

Yield: 6 servings (1½ cups each)
1 serving = 1 teaspoon oil

Stuffed Tomatoes

- 6 ripe tomatoes
- 2 teaspoons salt
- 1 teaspoon pepper
- 1 tablespoon oil
- ¼ cup chopped green pepper
- 5 tablespoons chopped green onions
- 1½ cups firm-cooked rice
- ½ cup mayonnaise-type salad dressing

Cut off top of tomatoes; scoop out centers. Sprinkle the shells with the salt and pepper. Turn upside down to drain. Sauté the green pepper and green onions in the oil until soft. Combine with rice and salad dressing. Fill the tomato cavities with this mixture and chill before serving.

Yield: 6 servings
    1 serving = 1½ teaspoons oil

Herb Seasoned Broccoli

- 1 10-ounce package frozen broccoli spears
- ½ cup hot water
- 1 teaspoon chicken flavored bouillon granules
- ½ teaspoon marjoram leaves
- ½ teaspoon basil leaves
- ¼ teaspoon onion powder or 1 teaspoon minced onion
- dash nutmeg

Place broccoli in saucepan. Combine water with bouillon granules; pour over broccoli, and sprinkle with seasonings. Cover and bring to boil; separate spears with fork. Simmer 6 minutes or until tender; drain.

Yield: 4 servings

Okra with Tomatoes

- 1 pound fresh okra or 1 package frozen okra
- 1 tablespoon margarine
- 1 medium-sized onion, chopped
- 1½ cups drained canned tomatoes or 3 medium fresh tomatoes
- ½ teaspoon salt
- ½ teaspoon pepper
- 4 drops hot sauce (optional)

Remove stems from the fresh okra and wash well; cut in ½-inch slices (cut frozen okra while still frozen). Heat margarine in a large saucepan or in a frying pan with a tight fitting lid. Add the okra and onion to the pan and cook over medium heat, stirring frequently, until onion starts to brown (okra will not brown). Remove from heat; add tomatoes and pepper. Return to heat, bring to boil. Reduce heat, cover, and simmer slowly until the okra is tender (5-10 minutes). Serve immediately.

Yield: 6 servings (¾ cup each)
    1 serving = ½ teaspoon margarine

Super Carrots

- 2 tablespoons chopped onion
- 1 tablespoon chopped fresh parsley
- 2 tablespoons margarine
- 8 medium carrots, cut in 1½-inch pieces (approximately 4 cups)
- 1 10¾-ounce can beef consommé
- dash nutmeg

In a saucepan, sauté onion and parsley in margarine 5 minutes. Add carrots, consommé, and nutmeg. Cover and simmer over medium heat for 25 minutes. Uncover and cook 5-10 minutes more or until carrots are tender.

Yield: 6 servings (¾ cup each)
    1 serving = 1 teaspoon margarine

Spinach, Chinese Style

- 1 pound fresh spinach
- 1 tablespoon oil
- 1 clove garlic, crushed and minced
- ¼ teaspoon salt
- ½ teaspoon sugar
  dash ground black pepper (optional)
  dash MSG (optional)

Wash and drain spinach, removing wilted leaves. Heat oil and stir-fry garlic over high flame. Add spinach and quickly stir until oil is thoroughly mixed with the spinach. Add salt, sugar, MSG, and pepper. Stir again and cook uncovered for 1½-2 minutes.

Note: Since spinach cooks for only a short time, try to cook it at the very end of the meal preparation so that it will retain its tenderness and green color. All leafy vegetables such as watercress, lettuce, celery, cabbage, and Chinese greens (such as bok choy) can be cooked the same way.

Yield: 4 servings (approximately ½ cup each)
1 serving = ¾ teaspoon oil

Savory Cauliflower

- 1 medium head cauliflower (about 1¼ pounds)
- 2 tablespoons margarine, melted
- 4 tablespoons grated Parmesan cheese
- 1 teaspoon dried dill weed
- ⅛ teaspoon garlic powder (or 1 clove garlic, minced or mashed)
  salt and pepper to taste

Cut cauliflower into flowerettes and wash. Place in boiling water (enough to cover) and cook until tender. Drain and turn into a 2-quart baking dish. Mix margarine, 2 tablespoons of the Parmesan cheese, dill weed, and garlic together; mix with the hot cauliflower. Season to taste with salt and pepper. Sprinkle with the remaining Parmesan cheese and place under broiler, about 6 inches from heat, for about 10 minutes or until top is golden brown.

Yield: 8 servings (½ cup each)
1 serving = ¾ teaspoon margarine

Breads

Fabulous Fluffy Roll Dough

- 1 package active dry yeast
- ¼ cup warm (105-115°F.) water
- 1 cup skim milk, scalded (150°F.) then cooled to room temperature (80°F.)
- ½ cup sugar
- 1 teaspoon salt
- ⅓ cup oil
- ½ teaspoon baking soda
- 1 whole egg, slightly beaten
- 4½ - 5 cups unsifted all-purpose flour

In a large mixing bowl, disperse yeast in water by stirring. Add cooled skim milk, sugar, and salt; stir. Combine oil, soda, and eggs; add to yeast mixture, mixing well. Gradually stir in 4¼ cups flour and knead dough in bowl 15 strokes. Place in plastic bag and refrigerate 24 hours. Punch dough down; let rise 10 minutes, then knead 8 minutes on lightly floured surface.

Use this recipe for preparing Montmorency Cherry Coffee Cake and Maple Pecan Sweet Rolls.

Montmorency Cherry Coffee Cake

- ½ recipe Fabulous Fluffy Roll Dough
- ½ of a 21-ounce can cherry pie filling
- ¼ cup toasted slivered almonds
- ¼ cup powdered sugar
- 1 teaspoon skim milk

Set aside one-eighth of the dough to be used in this recipe. Roll remaining dough into an 8-inch square. Place in a lightly oiled 8-inch square pan. Combine cherry pie filling and almonds; spread over top of dough. Roll reserved dough into a 6-inch square; cut ten strips. Place strips on top of filling; interweave to form lattice. Let coffee cake rise in a warm place, free of drafts, for 30 minutes. Bake in a preheated 375°F. oven for 25-30 minutes. Cool. Prepare glaze by mixing together powdered sugar and skim milk. Drizzle over lattice pieces only.

Yield: 9 servings
1 serving = 1 teaspoon oil

Maple Pecan Sweet Rolls

- ⅓ cup chopped pecans
- ¼ cup maple-flavored pancake syrup
- ⅓ cup firmly packed light brown sugar
- 2 tablespoons margarine, divided
- ½ recipe Fabulous Fluffy Roll Dough
- ¼ cup firmly packed light brown sugar ground cinnamon (optional)

Place pecans in bottom of an oiled 8-inch square pan. Pour pancake syrup over nuts; sprinkle ⅓ cup brown sugar evenly over nuts and syrup. Melt 1 tablespoon margarine and drizzle over all else. Roll dough out to 9 x 7-inch rectangle. Spread with 1 tablespoon margarine and then sprinkle with ¼ cup brown sugar and, if desired, cinnamon. Roll up starting from 9-inch side, as with jelly roll. Seal edges well. Slice into 9 1-inch thick pieces. Place cut side up in pan. Cover; let rise in a warm place, free of drafts, until doubled in volume (about 45 minutes). Bake in a preheated 400°F. oven for 25 minutes or until done. Cool on rack 5-10 minutes, then invert into a plate.

Yield: 9 rolls
1 roll = 1 teaspoon oil
½ teaspoon margarine

Jewish Sour Rye Bread

- 2 packages active dry yeast, divided
- 1½ cups warm water (105-115°F.)
- 2 cups unsifted medium rye flour
- 1 cup beer, room temperature, measured after foam subsides
- 1 tablespoon sugar
- 3 tablespoons caraway seed, divided
- 1 tablespoon salt
- 6½ - 7 cups unsifted all-purpose flour
- 3 egg whites, divided
- 3 tablespoons margarine
- 2 teaspoons water
- caraway seed for top

In a medium-sized mixing bowl, disperse 1 package of yeast in warm water. Add rye flour, and stir together well; cover bowl tightly with plastic wrap. Let stand at room temperature *3 days* and *3 nights*. This makes the starter. On the 4th day, pour all of starter into large mixing bowl. Add 1 package yeast and beer; mix well with electric mixer. Add sugar, 2 tablespoons caraway seed, salt, 2 cups all-purpose flour, and 2 egg whites. Beat at medium speed for 2 minutes. Add margarine and beat 2 more minutes. Stir in 4-5 cups all-purpose flour. Cover dough with plastic wrap and let rest 10 minutes. Turn out onto lightly floured board. Knead dough about 8 minutes, adding approximately ½ cup all-purpose flour. Transfer to a large lightly oiled bowl; cover top with plastic wrap and slit wrap in 2 places with sharp knife. Allow to rise until doubled in volume (approximately 60 minutes). At end of first rising, punch down dough. Turn out onto a lightly floured surface; cut into three equal pieces. With lightly floured rolling pin, roll each piece out to a 12 x 8-inch rectangle. Sprinkle each with 1 teaspoon caraway seeds. Starting from 8-inch side, roll up dough tightly; seal each turn. Pinch "seam" together; tuck ends under and roll 2-3 times to give loaf even shape. Place three loaves well apart on lightly oiled cookie sheets. Cover and let rise again until doubled in volume (about 45 minutes). Just before baking slash top of each loaf diagonally in 3 or 4 equidistant places. In a small bowl mix 1 egg white with 5 teaspoons water. With a pastry brush, brush tops and sides of loaves, being careful not to let it run down into the pan. Sprinkle the loaves with a small amount of caraway seed. Bake at 350°F. for 35-45 minutes. Cool on wire racks.

Yield: 3 loaves
    1 loaf = 3 tablespoons margarine

Dilly Bread

- 1 package active dry yeast
- ½ cup warm (105-115°F.) water
- 1 cup low-fat (2%) cottage cheese
- 1 tablespoon instant minced onion
- 1 tablespoon dill seed
- 1 whole egg, beaten
- 2 tablespoons sugar
- 1 teaspoon salt
- ¼ teaspoon baking soda
- 3½ cups sifted all-purpose flour
- 1 tablespoon margarine, melted
- salt

In a large mixing bowl, disperse yeast in water by stirring. Warm cottage cheese over low heat to room temperature (80°F.), stirring often. Add cottage cheese to yeast mixture. Mix in remaining ingredients except for flour, margarine, and salt. Gradually stir in 3 cups flour until a stiff dough is formed. Cover bowl with plastic wrap; make a single slit in wrap. Let dough rise approximately 60 minutes. Turn out onto a lightly floured board and knead in remaining flour as needed. Dough is properly kneaded when it becomes smooth and satiny and small blisters of air can be seen just beneath the surface. Shape into two loaves and place in 9 x 5 x 3-inch pans. Let rise until doubled in volume. Bake in a preheated oven for 45-50 minutes. Remove from pan and cool on rack. While warm, brush loaves with margarine and sprinkle with salt. Loaves freeze well.

Yield: 2 loaves
    1 loaf = ½ egg
           1½ teaspoons margarine

Greek Easter Bread

- 2 packages active dry yeast
- ¼ cup warm (105-115°F.)
- ¾ cup skim milk
- ½ cup margarine
- 4 whole eggs
- ½ teaspoon salt
- ½ cup sugar
- 1 teaspoon ground cinnamon
- ½ teaspoon ground nutmeg
- 5½ - 6 cups sifted all-purpose flour
- 1 hard-cooked egg, dyed red in the shell
- 1 egg white, slightly beaten sesame seeds

In large mixing bowl, stir yeast into water to hydrate yeast. Heat milk and margarine together until milk is scalded (about 150°F.); cool to room temperature (about 80°F.). Add milk to yeast in large bowl. Add eggs, one at a time, beating well. Add salt and sugar, mix until dissolved. Add cinnamon, nutmeg, and 2 cups sifted flour. Beat batter at medium speed with electric mixer for 5 minutes. Gradually stir in remaining flour.

Allow dough to rest for 10 minutes in a covered bowl. Turn out onto a floured board and knead until smooth and elastic (about 10 minutes). Add flour as needed. Dough is properly kneaded when small blisters of air can be seen just beneath the surface. Place dough in oiled mixing bowl, turning once to oil top of dough. Permit dough to rise for approximately 1½ hours or until doubled in volume. Punch down; turn out onto a very lightly floured surface and knead gently 2-3 times.

Cut off a small piece (about one-tenth of dough); reserve. Shape remaining dough into a single large round loaf. Place on a lightly oiled baking sheet. In the center, place one red dyed egg. Shape reserved dough into two pencil-thin strips; place strips on top of egg in the shape of a cross. Press ends into loaf to secure egg. Cover and permit to rise until doubled in volume. Brush loaf with slightly beaten egg white and sprinkle with sesame seeds. Bake in a preheated 325°F. oven for 50-55 minutes or until loaf sounds hollow when thumped. Serve warm, or cool on a rack.

Yield: 16 servings
    1 serving = ¼ egg
              1½ teaspoons margarine

Hot Cross Buns

- ¾ cup scalded whole milk
- ½ cup margarine
- ⅓ cup sugar
- 1 teaspoon salt
- ¼ cup warm water
- 1 package active dry yeast
- 1 egg, beaten
- ¾ cup currants
- ½ teaspoon mace
- 3½ - 4 cups sifted all-purpose flour vegetable oil
- 1 egg white, slightly beaten
- 1 cup confectioner's sugar
- 2 tablespoons hot water
- ½ teaspoon vanilla extract

In a large bowl, combine milk, margarine, sugar, and salt; cool to lukewarm. In a small bowl, sprinkle yeast in warm water and stir until dissolved. Add egg, currants, and mace to milk mixture. Add as much flour as can be stirred into dough — about 3½ cups.

Place in a greased clean bowl. Brush top with oil. Cover with a clean towel; let rise in a warm place (80°F.-85°F.) until doubled in bulk — about 2 hours.

Turn onto lightly floured surface; knead 1 minute; shape into 18 2-inch balls. In each of 2 greased 8 x 8 x 2-inch pans, arrange 9 balls, about 1 inch apart. With greased scissors, snip deep cross in each bun. Brush with egg white. Cover with towel; let rise second time in warm place until doubled in bulk. Preheat oven to 425°F. Bake buns 25 minutes or until done. Cool on wire rack; fill in the cross on each bun with combined confectioner's sugar, hot water, and vanilla extract.

Yield: 1½ dozen buns
    1 serving = 1⅓ teaspoons margarine

Brown Bread

1¼ cups packed dark brown sugar
1 whole egg
3 cups unsifted whole wheat flour or graham flour
1 teaspoon salt
2 teaspoons baking soda
2 cups buttermilk
1¾ cups dark seedless raisins

Blend brown sugar with egg. Combine whole wheat flour, salt, and soda; mix well. Stir dry ingredients alternately with buttermilk into sugar mixture. Add raisins. Turn into four 1-pound (#303 size) cans that have been lightly but thoroughly oiled. Fill cans one-half full. Bake in a preheated 350°F. oven for 40-45 minutes or until toothpick inserted in center comes out clean. Cool 5 minutes, then remove from can; cut out bottom if necessary. Cool on wire racks. Store in airtight container or freeze.

Yield: 4 loaves
1 loaf = ¼ egg

Healthful Bran Bread

2 cups sifted all-purpose flour
½ cup sugar
½ teaspoon salt
3 teaspoons baking powder
1¼ teaspoons baking soda
2 cups whole bran cereal
½ cup molasses
2 cups plus 2 tablespoons cultured buttermilk
2 cups dark raisins

Sift together flour, sugar, salt, baking powder, and soda into a large mixing bowl. Stir in whole bran cereal. In center of dry ingredients, make a well. In separate bowl, mix together remaining ingredients. Add all at once to dry mixture; stir until well blended. Turn into two lightly oiled 9 x 5 x 3-inch loaf pans. Bake in a preheated 350°F. oven for 30-40 minutes. Cool in pan 5 minutes, then turn out onto rack. Slice when cool.

Yield: 2 9-inch loaves

Beer Bread

3 cups sifted self-rising flour
3 tablespoons sugar
1 12-ounce can beer, room temperature

Combine ingredients in large mixing bowl; mix well by hand with heavy spoon. Turn into a lightly oiled 9 x 5 x 3-inch loaf pan. Bake in a preheated 350°F. oven for 60 minutes. Remove from pan and cool on wire rack.

Yield: 1 loaf

Cranberry Nut Loaf

1 16-ounce can whole berry cranberry sauce
2 cups sifted all-purpose flour
1½ teaspoons baking powder
½ teaspoon baking soda
1 teaspoon salt
1 whole egg
2 tablespoons oil
¾ cup sugar
¼ cup orange juice
2 1x2-inch pieces orange rind
¼ cup chopped pecans

Empty cranberry sauce into small saucepan and warm over low heat until liquid portion is thin enough to pass through a sieve. Strain; reserve ½ cup liquid and all of whole berries. Sift together flour, baking powder, soda, and salt into large mixing bowl. Make well in center of dry ingredients. Place egg, oil, sugar, reserved ½ cup of cranberry liquid, orange juice, and orange rind into a blender container. Cover and process until rind is grated fine. Add nuts and process just enough to mix. Add to flour mixture and gently stir until dry ingredients are *almost* moistened. Fold in reserved whole cranberries. Turn into one lightly oiled 9 x 5 x 3-inch loaf pan. Bake in a preheated 350°F. oven for 50-55 minutes or until loaf springs back when lightly touched in center.

Yield: 12 servings
1 serving = ½ teaspoon oil

Blueberry Pecan Bread

- 1¾ cups sifted all-purpose flour
- ⅔ cup sugar
- 1½ teaspoons baking powder
- ½ teaspoon salt
- ½ teaspoon baking soda
- 2 teaspoons grated orange rind
- ⅓ cup orange juice
- 2 tablespoons oil
- ½ cup (approximately) water
- ¾ cup pecans, chopped
- 2 tablespoons unsifted all-purpose flour
- 1 cup fresh blueberries, washed and dried (do not use canned or frozen)

Sift together flour, sugar, baking powder, soda, and salt; place in a large mixing bowl. Make a well in center of dry ingredients. In a one-cup measuring cup, combine rind, orange juice, and oil. Add enough water to measure 1 cup. Add this mixture all at once to dry ingredients; stir. In a separate bowl, combine pecans, flour, and blueberries; add this mixture to batter. Mix well, being careful not to mash berries. Place batter in a lightly oiled 9 x 5 x 3-inch loaf pan. Bake in a preheated 350°F. oven for 50-55 minutes or until a toothpick inserted in center comes out clean. Remove bread from pan; cool on rack. Store in an airtight container.

Yield: 18 slices
1 slice = ⅓ teaspoon oil

Apricot-Orange Bread

- 1 cup finely chopped dried apricots
- 2 cups water
- 2 tablespoons margarine
- 1 cup sugar
- 2 egg whites
- 1 tablespoon grated orange peel
- 3½ cups sifted all-purpose flour
- 2 teaspoons baking powder
- 1 teaspoon baking soda
- 1 teaspoon salt
- ½ cup instant nonfat dry milk powder
- ½ cup orange juice
- ½ cup chopped pecans

In medium-sized saucepan, combine apricots and water; cook 10-15 minutes or until tender but not mushy. Drain liquid, reserving ¾ cup. Set apricots aside to cool. Cream together margarine and sugar; beat in egg whites and grated orange peel by hand. Sift together flour, baking powder, soda, salt, and dry milk. Add to creamed mixture alternately with reserved apricot liquid and orange juice. Stir apricot pieces and pecans into batter. Turn into two lightly oiled 9 x 5 x 3-inch loaf pans. Bake in a preheated 350°F. oven for 40-45 minutes or until bread springs back when lightly touched in center.

Yield: 2 9-inch loaves
1 loaf = 3 teaspoons margarine

Banana Nut Bread

- 1½ cups mashed ripe bananas
- ½ cup cultured buttermilk
- 1 teaspoon vanilla
- ¼ cup margarine
- 1 cup firmly packed light brown sugar
- 2 whole eggs
- 2 cups sifted all-purpose flour
- 1 teaspoon baking soda
- 1 teaspoon salt
- ½ cup chopped pecans

Combine mashed bananas with buttermilk and vanilla; set aside. Cream margarine and brown sugar together until light. By hand, beat in eggs, one at a time. Add banana mixture; beat well. Sift together flour, soda, and salt; add all at once to liquid. Stir until well blended. Fold in nuts. Turn into two lightly oiled 9 x 5 x 3-inch loaf pans. Bake in a preheated 350°F. oven for 50-55 minutes or until toothpick inserted in center comes out clean. Cool 5 minutes in pan, then turn out. Wrap when cool and store 24 hours at room temperature before serving.

Yield: 24 servings
1 serving = ¼ teaspoon margarine

Pecan Nut Bread

- 2½ cups sifted all-purpose flour
- 1 cup sugar
- 3½ teaspoons baking powder
- 1 teaspoon salt
- 3 tablespoons oil
- 1¼ cups skim milk
- 1 whole egg, slightly beaten
- 1 cup chopped pecans

Sift together flour, sugar, baking powder, and salt into a large mixing bowl. In center of dry ingredients, make well. Combine remaining ingredients; add all at once to flour mixture. Beat with electric mixer on medium speed for 30 seconds. Turn into a lightly oiled 9 x 5 x 3-inch loaf pan. Bake in a preheated 350°F. oven for 40-50 minutes or until toothpick inserted in center comes out clean. Cool 5 minutes in pan, then turn out onto rack. When cool, wrap and then store 24 hours at room temperature before eating.

Yield: 18 servings
1 serving = ½ teaspoon oil

Zucchini Bread

- 3 cups sifted all-purpose flour
- 1 cup sugar
- 2 teaspoons baking powder
- ½ teaspoon baking soda
- 1 teaspoon salt
- 3 teaspoons ground cinnamon
- 2 eggs, beaten
- ½ cup water
- ¼ cup oil
- 2 teaspoons vanilla
- 2 cups finely shredded zucchini (peeled or unpeeled, as preferred)
- ½ cup chopped pecans
- ½ cup dark raisins

Combine dry ingredients in a large mixing bowl; mix well and make well in center. In separate bowl, mix together remaining ingredients; add this mixture all at once to dry ingredients. Stir just enough to moisten dry ingredients. Turn into two lightly oiled 9 x 5 x 3-inch loaf pans. Bake in a preheated 350°F. oven for 50-55 minutes or until toothpick inserted in center comes out clean. Cool 5 minutes in pan, then turn out onto rack. Wrap when cool, and store 24 hours at room temperature before eating.

Yield: 24 servings
1 serving = 1 teaspoon oil

Pumpkin Bread

- ½ cup oil
- 3 whole eggs
- ⅔ cup water
- 1 16-ounce can pumpkin
- 3 cups sugar, divided
- 3½ cups sifted all-purpose flour
- 1½ teaspoons salt
- 1¼ teaspoons ground nutmeg
- 1¼ teaspoons ground cinnamon
- 2 teaspoons baking soda
- 1 cup golden raisins
- ½ cup chopped pecans

In large mixing bowl; blend together by hand: oil, eggs, water, pumpkin, and 2 cups of sugar. Sift together remaining cup of sugar, flour, salt, nutmeg, cinnamon, and soda into separate medium-sized bowl; stir until well mixed. Stir dry ingredients into pumpkin mixture until just a few streaks of flour can be seen. Add raisins and pecans; continue stirring until batter is mixed, but do not overstir. Turn into two lightly oiled 9 x 5 x 3-inch loaf pans. Bake in a preheated 325°F. oven for 65-70 minutes or until toothpick inserted in center comes out clean.

Yield: 32 servings (½-inch slice)
1 serving = ¾ teaspoon oil

Honey Pineapple Bread

- 2 tablespoons oil
- 1 cup honey
- 2 egg whites, slightly beaten
- 2 cups unsifted all-purpose flour
- 2 teaspoons baking powder
- ¾ teaspoon salt
- 1 cup bran
- 1 cup pineapple juice
- ½ cup chopped pecans

In a large mixing bowl, blend together oil, honey, and egg whites. Stir flour, baking powder, salt, and bran together in separate bowl. Add flour mixture and pineapple juice all at once to honey mixture; stir until dry ingredients are just moistened. Fold in nuts. Turn batter into a lightly oiled 9 x 5 x 3-inch loaf pan. Bake in a preheated 350°F. oven for 50-60 minutes or until bread begins to pull away from sides of pan.

Yield: 12 servings
  1 serving = ½ teaspoon oil

Blueberry Coffee Cake

- ½ cup sugar
- 1¼ cups sifted all-purpose flour
- 2 teaspoons baking powder
- ½ teaspoon salt
- 3 tablespoons margarine, melted
- ½ cup skim milk
- 1 whole egg, well beaten
- 1½ cups blueberries, fresh or frozen (if fresh, washed and dried)
- 2 tablespoons sugar
- ⅓ cup chopped pecans

Sift together ½ cup sugar, flour, baking powder, and salt into a large bowl. Mix melted margarine into flour mixture until all particles are coated with a layer of fat. Make a well in center. Combine milk and egg; add all at once to flour mixture. Stir until dry ingredients are moistened and liquid is evenly distributed. Turn into a lightly oiled 8-inch baking pan. Sprinkle blueberries and sugar over top of batter. Bake in a preheated 350°F. oven for 30 minutes.

Without removing coffee cake from oven, top evenly with nuts. Bake an additional 5-10 minutes or until toothpick inserted in center comes out clean.

Yield: 9 servings
  1 serving = 1 teaspoon margarine

One-Step Tropical Coffee Cake

- ¼ cup firmly packed light brown sugar
- 3 tablespoons all-purpose flour
- ¾ teaspoon ground cinnamon
- 2 tablespoons margarine
- ⅓ cup slivered almonds
- 1½ cups sifted all-purpose flour
- 1 cup sugar
- 2 teaspoons baking powder
- ½ teaspoon salt
- 1 8-ounce carton fruit flavored low-fat yogurt*
- ¼ cup oil
- 2 whole eggs, slightly beaten

In small bowl, combine first five ingredients until crumbly; reserve for later use. In large mixing bowl, blend together last seven ingredients by beating 3 minutes with electric mixer at medium speed. Turn into a lightly oiled 8-inch square pan. Sprinkle reserved mixture over top of batter. Bake in a preheated 350°F. oven for 30-35 minutes or until toothpick inserted in center comes out clean. Cool in pan.

*Suggested flavors: pineapple, peach, lemon, or mandarin orange.

Yield: 12 servings
  1 serving = 1 teaspoon oil
         1 teaspoon margarine

Buttermilk Coffee Cake

2½ cups sifted all-purpose flour
1 cup firmly packed light brown sugar
¾ cup sugar
1 teaspoon ground cinnamon
½ teaspoon salt
½ cup oil
⅓ cup chopped pecans
1 teaspoon baking soda
1 teaspoon baking powder
2 egg whites, slightly beaten
1 cup cultured buttermilk

Combine flour, sugars, cinnamon, salt, and oil. Mix well. Remove ½ cup of mixture and add nuts to this for topping; reserve. To the remaining mixture, add soda and baking powder; mix together very well. Add egg whites and buttermilk. Beat with electric mixer on medium speed for 2 minutes. Turn into a lightly oiled tube pan (or 13 x 9 x 2-inch pan); sprinkle reserved topping over top. Bake in a preheated 350°F. oven for 35-40 minutes or until cake just begins to pull away from sides of pan. Freezes well.

Yield: 24 servings
1 serving = 1 teaspoon oil

Apple Coffee Cake

8 medium-sized apples, cored and finely chopped
2 cups sugar
2 teaspoons ground cinnamon
⅓ cup oil
2 whole eggs, well beaten
1 teaspoon salt
½ cup chopped pecans
1 cup dark raisins
2 teaspoons vanilla
2 cups sifted all-purpose flour
1½ teaspoons baking soda

In large mixing bowl, combine apples with sugar, cinnamon, oil, eggs, salt, pecans, raisins, and vanilla; mix well. Let stand 30 minutes. Sift together flour and soda. Stir into apple mixture. Turn into a lightly oiled 13 x 9 x 2-inch pan. Bake in a preheated 350°F. oven for 45-50 minutes. Cool in pan.

Yield: 16 servings
1 serving = 1 teaspoon oil

Christmas Coffee Cake

½ cup packed light brown sugar
1 tablespoon ground cinnamon
½ cup finely chopped pecans
1¾ cups sifted cake flour
1 teaspoon baking powder
½ teaspoon baking soda
¼ teaspoon salt
¼ cup margarine, softened
1 cup packed light brown sugar
1 whole egg
1 cup aged yogurt*

Combine ½ cup brown sugar, cinnamon, and pecans to make topping; reserve. Sift together flour, baking powder, soda, and salt. In a large mixing bowl, cream margarine and 1 cup brown sugar; add egg; beat well. Stir in yogurt alternately with presifted dry ingredients. Be careful not to overmix. Spread half of batter in a lightly oiled 8-inch square pan; cover with two-thirds of reserved nut mixture. Add remaining batter and sprinkle with remaining nut topping. Bake in a preheated 350°F. oven for 35-40 minutes. Cool in pan.

*Yogurt that is older than the expiration date works very well in this recipe. Yogurt remains safe to eat past the expiration date; however, the flavor becomes more pronounced with time.

Yield: 12 servings
1 serving = 1 teaspoon margarine

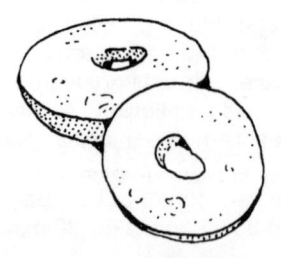

Fruitcake

- 1 cup packed brown sugar
- ¾ cup water
- 1 cup raisins
- 1½ cups chopped candied fruit
- ⅓ cup oil
- 1 teaspoon ground cinnamon
- ¼ teaspoon ground nutmeg
- ½ teaspoon ground cloves
- ¼ teaspoon salt
- 1 teaspoon baking soda
- 1 teaspoon baking powder
- 2 cups sifted flour
- ½ cup chopped pecans

Preheat oven to 350°F. Bring sugar, water, raisins, candied fruit, and oil to a boil and simmer for 5 minutes. Cool. Sift the spices, salt, baking powder, and baking soda together with the flour. Combine flour mixture with fruit mixture; mix well. Stir in the pecans. Turn into an oiled and floured 9 x 5-inch loaf pan. Bake for 50 minutes or until toothpick comes out clean. Remove from pan; cool before wrapping. Allow to stand at least 12 hours before slicing.

Yield: 16 servings
    1 serving = 1 teaspoon oil

Fruitless Fruitcake

- 2 cups seedless raisins
- 1½ cups sugar
- 1 cup cold water
- 1 teaspoon ground cloves
- 1 tablespoon ground cinnamon
- ½ teaspoon salt
- ½ cup oil
- 2 whole eggs
- 1 cup chopped pecans
- 1 teaspoon baking soda dissolved in ½ teaspoon water
- 2½ cups sifted all-purpose flour

Mix the first six ingredients together in a saucepan and cook until the raisins become plump. Mix the remaining ingredients together and combine with the raisin mixture. Turn the mixture into a 10-inch tube pan which has been greased and dusted with flour. Bake at 350°F. for about 60 minutes.

This cake is very good soaked in brandy, rum, or a mixture of the two. To do this, place the cake, after it has cooled, into a container which can be tightly closed. Pour 2 ounces of brandy slowly over the cake so as to allow it to soak in. You may add more or less brandy, depending on your taste. Close the container tightly. Keep cake in container for approximately three weeks, turning it over once a week so that the brandy will not settle at the bottom of the cake. The cake can be stored for quite a long period of time after it has been soaked. If the cake is to be stored for a long time, you should continue to turn it periodically.

Yield: 16 servings
    1 serving = 1½ teaspoons oil
    ⅛ egg

Matzo Bagels

- ¾ cup margarine (or ¾ cup oil)
- 3 cups matzo meal
- 1 teaspoon salt
- 6 whole eggs

Melt margarine and pour over mixture of matzo meal and salt. Beat eggs and add to matzo meal mixture. Mix well. On greased cookie sheet, form rounds 3 inches in diameter and ½ inch deep; make a hole in the center, if desired. Bake at 425°F. for 35 minutes.

One can bake the whole recipe, or bake half and refrigerate the rest of the batter. It will keep for several days in a closed container.

Yield: 2 dozen
    1 bagel = ¼ of an egg
    1½ teaspoons margarine

Whole Wheat Pineapple Muffins

- 1 8-ounce can crushed pineapple, packed in own juice
- 1 cup whole wheat flour
- 1 cup sifted all-purpose flour
- 2¼ teaspoons baking powder
- ¼ teaspoon soda
- ½ teaspoon salt
- ¼ cup sugar
- ¼ cup oil
- 1 whole egg
- orange juice, approximately ½ cup

Drain pineapple; reserve liquid. Place whole wheat flour in large mixing bowl. Sift together remaining dry ingredients and add to whole wheat flour. Add orange juice to liquid drained from pineapple juice to make ¾ cup and combine with oil and egg. Make well in center of dry ingredients; add liquid mixture all at once. Stir until dry ingredients are moistened. Do not overmix. Fill lightly oiled muffin tins two-thirds full. Bake in a preheated 400°F. oven for 15-20 minutes. Remove from pans; serve hot.

Yield: 12 muffins
1 muffin = 1 teaspoon oil

Six-Week Bran Muffins

- 1 15-ounce box raisin bran cereal
- 3 cups sugar
- 5 cups sifted all-purpose flour
- 2 teaspoons baking soda
- 1 teaspoon baking powder
- 2 teaspoons salt
- 2 teaspoons ground nutmeg
- 4 teaspoons ground cinnamon
- 1 cup oil
- 3 whole eggs, well beaten
- 1 quart cultured buttermilk

Into a very large mixing bowl, empty box of raisin bran. Sift together sugar, flour, soda, baking powder, salt, nutmeg, and cinnamon into same bowl, mix well. In a separate bowl, combine remaining ingredients and add to dry ingredients; stir just enough to moisten and evenly distribute liquid. Store in an airtight container; will keep in refrigerator for up to 6 weeks. To bake, fill lightly oiled muffin tins two-thirds full. Bake in a preheated 400°F. oven for 18-20 minutes.

Yield: 40 muffins
1 muffin = 1 teaspoon oil

Date and Orange Muffins

- 1 whole seedless orange
- ½ cup orange juice
- ½ cup dates, pitted and chopped
- 1 egg
- ½ cup margarine
- 1½ cups all-purpose flour
- 1 teaspoon baking soda
- 1 teaspoon baking powder
- ¾ cup sugar
- 1 scant teaspoon salt

Without peeling orange, cut into pieces and drop into blender. Blend until rind is finely ground. Add juice, dates, egg, and margarine and give another whirl in the blender. Into a bowl, sift flour, baking soda, baking powder, sugar, and salt. Pour orange mixture over dry ingredients and stir lightly. Divide mixture among eighteen greased muffin tins and bake in a 400°F. oven about 15 minutes.

Yield: 18 muffins
1 muffin = 1½ teaspoons margarine

Oatmeal Muffins

1⅓ cups old-fashioned rolled oats
1⅓ cups buttermilk
1⅓ cups sifted all-purpose flour
½ cup sugar
½ teaspoon baking soda
1 teaspoon baking powder
½ teaspoon salt
1 whole egg, well beaten
2 tablespoons oil

Combine rolled oats with buttermilk; let stand 15 minutes. Sift flour, sugar, baking soda, baking powder, and salt together into a large mixing bowl. Make well in center of dry ingredients. Combine egg and oil with oat-buttermilk mixture. Add all at once to dry ingredients, stirring just until barely moistened. Fill lightly oiled muffin tins two-thirds full. Bake in a preheated 400°F. oven for 17-20 minutes.

Yield: 12 muffins
1 muffin = ½ teaspoon oil

Blueberry Muffins

2 tablespoons margarine
¾ cup sugar
1 whole egg
1½ cups sifted cake flour
½ teaspoon salt
2 teaspoons baking powder
½ cup skim milk
1 cup blueberries, fresh or frozen (if fresh, washed and dried)

In a large bowl, cream together margarine and sugar; add egg and beat well by hand. Stir in sifted dry ingredients alternately with milk; mix together until blended. Fill lightly oiled muffin tins two-thirds full. Place 1 teaspoon blueberries on top of batter for each muffin. Bake in a preheated 375°F. oven for 15-20 minutes or until toothpick inserted in center of muffin comes out clean.

Yield: 11 muffins
1 muffin = ½ teaspoon margarine

Corn Bread

1 cup sifted all-purpose flour
¾ cup yellow cornmeal
½ teaspoon salt
2½ teaspoons baking powder
2 tablespoons sugar
1 egg white
2 tablespoons oil
1 cup skim milk

Sift together flour, cornmeal, salt, baking powder, and sugar into a medium-sized mixing bowl. Combine egg white, oil, and milk. Make well in center of dry ingredients; add liquid all at once. Stir until dry ingredients are moistened. Do not overmix. Turn into a lightly oiled 8-inch square pan. Bake in preheated 425°F. oven for 20 minutes or until toothpick inserted in center comes out clean.

Yield: 12 servings
1 serving = ½ teaspoon oil

Easy Spoon Bread

2 cups white cornmeal
1 teaspoon salt
2 cups boiling water
2 tablespoons margarine
1½ cups skim milk
2 whole eggs, well beaten
2 egg whites

Using a medium-sized mixing bowl, stir together cornmeal, salt, boiling water, and margarine. Continue stirring until margarine melts. Add milk; beat until smooth with electric mixer set at medium speed. Stir in whole eggs. In a small mixing bowl, beat egg whites until stiff. Gently fold egg whites into cornmeal mixture. Turn into a lightly oiled 2-quart souffle dish. Bake in a preheated 375°F. oven for 60-65 minutes or until puffy and golden brown. Do not overbake. Serve at once.

Yield: 8 servings
1 serving = ¼ egg
¾ teaspoon margarine

Master Mix

- 9 cups sifted all-purpose flour
- 1/3 cup baking powder
- 4 teaspoons salt
- 1/4 cup sugar
- 1 teaspoon cream of tartar
- 1 cup nonfat dry milk solids
- 1 cup oil

Using a very large mixing bowl, sift together flour, baking powder, salt, cream of tartar, and dry milk; sift again. With pastry blender, cut in oil until mixture is consistency of corn meal. Store in tightly covered container at room temperature. Mix will keep for six weeks. To measure Master Mix, pile mix lightly into cup and level with spatula.

Yield: 13½ cups
1 cup = 4 teaspoons oil

Coffee Cake with Preserves (made from Master Mix)

Cake:
- 3 cups Master Mix
- 1/2 cup sugar
- 3/4 cup water
- 1 whole egg, slightly beaten

Filling:
- 1/2 cup preserves (any flavor)

Topping:
- 1 tablespoon sugar
- 1 tablespoon slivered almonds

In a large mixing bowl, combine Master Mix with sugar. Make a well in center of dry mixture. In a separate bowl, combine water and egg. Add all at once to dry ingredients; stir until flour is just moistened. Turn one-third of batter into a lightly oiled 8 x 8 x 2-inch baking pan. Spread 1/4 cup of preserves over batter. Repeat layers. Cover with last one-third of batter. Sprinkle 1 tablespoon sugar over top. Bake in preheated 400°F. oven for 15 minutes. Sprinkle slivered almonds on top of partially baked cake and return to oven for 10-20 minutes longer or until toothpick inserted in center comes out clean. Cool in pan on rack.

Yield: 10 servings
1 serving = 1 teaspoon oil

Biscuits (made from Master Mix)

- 3¼ cups Master Mix
- 1/8 teaspoon baking soda
- 2/3 cup skim milk

Place Master Mix in a large mixing bowl; make a well in center. Add baking soda to milk; stir to dissolve. Add milk and soda mixture all at once to Master Mix. Stir with a fork just until dough follows fork around bowl. Turn onto lightly floured surface; knead gently 5 strokes. Roll dough one-half inch thick. Cut with 2-inch biscuit cutter dipped in flour. Place on unoiled baking sheet; bake in a preheated 425°F. oven for 10 minutes.

Yield: 12 biscuits
1 biscuit = 1 teaspoon oil

Muffins (made from Master Mix)

- 3½ cups Master Mix
- 1/4 cup sugar
- 1 cup minus 1 tablespoon water
- 1 whole egg
- 3 teaspoons sesame seeds, toasted

Place Master Mix in large mixing bowl; add sugar and stir well. In center of dry ingredients, make a well. In a separate bowl, combine water and egg. Add all at once to dry ingredients; stir until flour is just moistened and liquid is evenly distributed. Fill lightly oiled muffin tins two-thirds full. Top each muffin with 1/4 teaspoon toasted sesame seeds. Bake in a preheated 425°F. oven for 15-20 minutes.

Yield: 12 muffins
1 muffin = 1 teaspoon oil

Pancakes (made from Master Mix)

- 3 cups Master Mix
- 1⅓ cups water
- 1 whole egg, separated
- 1 tablespoon plus 1 teaspoon oil

Place Master Mix in large mixing bowl; in center, make a well. In a separate bowl, combine water and egg yolk. Add all at once to Master Mix; stir until flour is just moistened. Whip egg white to soft peak stage; fold whipped egg white into batter. (For runnier batter, add 1-2 tablespoons additional water to the batter.) Bake on a hot griddle, using 1 teaspoon oil for every four pancakes.

Yield: 16 4-inch pancakes
1 pancake = 1 teaspoon oil

Waffles (made from Master Mix)

Add 1 tablespoon plus 2 teaspoons water to batter for pancakes; gently mix in.

Note: Do not add fat of any sort to waffle iron after it is seasoned. Should waffles stick, turn up heat slightly.

Yield: 10 4-inch square waffles
1 waffle = 1 teaspoon oil

Easy Biscuits

- 1½ cups sifted all-purpose flour
- 2¼ teaspoons baking powder
- ½ teaspoon salt
- ¾ cup skim milk
- 3 tablespoons low-fat mayonnaise

Sift together flour, baking powder, and salt into a medium-sized bowl; make well in center. Combine skim milk and low-fat mayonnaise. Add all at once to dry ingredients. Stir until all flour is well moistened. Drop by heaping tablespoonsful onto a lightly oiled cookie sheet. Bake in a preheated 400°F. oven for 15-20 minutes or until golden brown. Remove from pan and serve hot.

Yield: 16 servings

Drop Cookies
(made from Master Mix)

- 3 cups Master Mix
- ½ cup sugar
- 1 whole egg
- ¼ cup water
- 1 teaspoon vanilla
- ½ cup dark raisins

Place Master Mix in a large mixing bowl; add sugar and stir well. In center of dry ingredients, make a well. In a separate bowl, combine egg, water, and vanilla. Add all at once to dry ingredients. Stir until water is absorbed and batter is formed. Gently fold in raisins. Drop from teaspoon onto a lightly oiled cookie sheet. Bake in a preheated 375°F. oven for 6-10 minutes or until top of cookie springs back when lightly touched.

Yield: 3 dozen cookies
1 cookie = ⅓ teaspoon oil

Orange Flavored Drop Cookies

Substitute ¼ cup plus 1 tablespoon buttermilk for ¼ cup water, and ½ cup chopped pecans for ½ cup raisins. To buttermilk, add 2 tablespoons finely grated orange peel. Method is same as for Drop Cookies.

Spice Drop Cookies

Add to Master Mix ½ teaspoon ground cinnamon, ⅛ teaspoon ground nutmeg, and ¼ teaspoon ground cardamon. Substitute ½ cup brown sugar for ½ cup white sugar. Decrease vanilla to ½ teaspoon. Method is same as for Drop Cookies.

Puffy French Toast

- 1 cup sifted all-purpose flour
- ½ teaspoon salt
- 1½ teaspoons baking powder
- 2 whole eggs
- 1 cup skim milk
- 8-10 slices fresh white bread
  cooking oil

Sift together flour, salt, and baking powder into a large, shallow pan. In a small bowl, blend eggs and skim milk. Add all at once to dry ingredients; mix well. Dip bread (may be cut in halves or thirds) in batter. Fry in 1 tablespoon oil in large skillet. Add more oil as needed, 1 teaspoon at a time. Drain on paper towel.

Yield: 8-10 servings
  1 serving = 1 teaspoon oil
  ¼ egg

Finnish Oven Pancake

- ¼ cup margarine
- ⅓ cup sugar
- 1 cup sifted all-purpose flour
- ¼ teaspoon salt
- 4 egg whites
- 2 cups skim milk

Melt margarine; set aside to cool. Sift together sugar, flour, and salt. In a medium-sized bowl using an electric mixer, beat egg whites until frothy. Alternately add dry ingredients and milk to egg white; beat well with electric mixer after each addition. Stir in melted margarine. Turn into a lightly oiled 13 x 9 x 2-inch pan. Bake in a preheated 375°F. oven for approximately 30 minutes or until edges of pancake are golden brown. Serve warm with preserves or syrup at breakfast or as a dessert.

Yield: 8 servings
  1 serving = 1½ teaspoons margarine

Cake Doughnuts

- 3⅓ cups sifted all-purpose flour, divided
- ⅞ cup sugar
- 3 teaspoons baking powder
- ½ teaspoon salt
- ½ teaspoon ground cinnamon
- ½ teaspoon ground nutmeg
- 2 tablespoons margarine, softened
- 2 whole eggs, well beaten
- ¾ cup skim milk
  cooking oil

Sift 1¼ cups of the flour with other dry ingredients into large mixing bowl. Add margarine, eggs, and skim milk. Beat for 30 seconds on low speed of electric mixer; scrape bowl as necessary. Beat for 1½ minutes longer on medium speed; scrape bowl occasionally. Add remaining flour, stirring just enough to mix. Turn dough onto well floured, cloth covered board; roll gently in flour. Roll dough out to ⅜-inch thickness. Cut out doughnuts with floured doughnut cutter. While doughnuts dry slightly, heat oil to 375°F. in deep fat fryer or in deep skillet. Oil should be 3-4 inches deep. Slip doughnuts into hot oil with wide spatula. Turn doughnuts as they rise to surface, then brown 2-3 minutes on each side or until golden brown. When removing doughnuts from oil, do not prick.

Yield: 1½ dozen doughnuts
  1 doughnut = 1 teaspoon oil
    ⅓ teaspoon margarine
    1/10 egg

Desserts

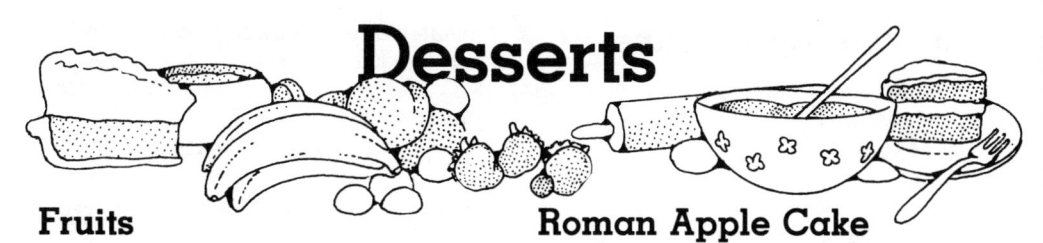

Fruits

Fruits are a lovely complement to any modified fat and cholesterol menu. Fresh fruits used as a dessert provide vitamins and minerals without accompanying high calories or fat. Use sugar sparingly or not at all.

The addition of fresh fruits to a meal requires little preparation time. This collection of recipes does not include a large number using fresh fruits, because fat and cholesterol are not a problem with this food group. You are encouraged to make your own collection of fresh fruit recipes from favorite cookbooks.

Remember to keep fresh fruit recipes simple. Avoid combination recipes using cream cheese, sour cream, non-dairy whipped toppings, whipped cream, and other high-cholesterol and high-fat products.

Fresh Apple Cake

- ⅔ cup oil
- 2 whole eggs
- 2 teaspoons vanilla
- 2 cups sugar
- 3 cups sifted flour
- 1½ teaspoons baking soda
- 1 teaspoon salt
- 3 cups pared and finely chopped raw apples
- 1 cup finely chopped pecans

Cream together oil, eggs, sugar, and vanilla. Sift flour, soda, and salt together. Add gradually to creamed mixture. Fold in chopped apples and nuts. Do not beat. Pour into a greased and floured 10-inch tube pan. Bake at 350°F. for 75 minutes. Cool at least 20 minutes before turning out.

Yield: 16 servings
  1 serving = ⅛ egg
              2 teaspoons oil

Roman Apple Cake

Topping:
- 1 tablespoon margarine, melted
- 2 teaspoons ground cinnamon
- ⅓ cup packed brown sugar
- 2 teaspoons unsifted flour
- ½ cup chopped pecans
- ¼ cup old-fashioned rolled oats

Cake:
- 1 cup sugar
- 2¼ cups sifted all-purpose flour
- ¼ teaspoon salt
- ½ teaspoon baking powder
- 1½ teaspoons baking soda
- ½ teaspoon ground cloves
- 1 teaspoon ground cinnamon
- 2 whole eggs
- ⅔ cup skim milk
- 1½ teaspoons vanilla
- ⅓ cup margarine, softened
- 3 cups pared and shredded raw apples

In a small mixing bowl, combine all ingredients for topping; set aside to be used later. Sift together sugar, flour, salt, baking powder, baking soda, cloves, and cinnamon; place in a large mixing bowl. Combine eggs, milk, and vanilla. Add margarine and ½ of milk mixture to dry ingredients; mix by beating 100 vigorous strokes by hand. Add remaining milk mixture and beat an additional 40 strokes by hand. Fold in apples. Turn into a lightly oiled 13 x 9-inch pan. Top with reserved nut and oat mixture. Bake in a moderate oven to 350°F. for 35-45 minutes.

Yield: 24 servings
  1 serving = ¾ teaspoon oil

Passover Apple Cake

- 1 cup matzo meal
- ½ teaspoon salt
- 5 egg whites
- ½ cup oil
- ¼ cup orange juice
- 1 cup sugar, divided
- ½ teaspoon ground cinnamon
- 4 cups thinly sliced apples (3-4 apples)

Stir the matzo meal and salt together, set aside. With electric mixer, beat 3 egg whites until stiff and set aside. Beat remaining 2 egg whites, oil, orange juice, and ¾ cup sugar together for 5 minutes. Stir in the stiffly beaten egg whites. Spoon half the batter into a greased 8-inch square pan. Arrange the apples over the batter. Mix the remaining ¼ cup sugar with the cinnamon and sprinkle over the apples. Spoon the rest of the batter over the apples. Bake at 375°F. for 35-40 minutes.

Yield: 8 servings
1 serving = 3 teaspoons oil

Applesauce Cake

- 1¾ cups sifted all-purpose flour
- 1⅓ cups sugar
- ¼ teaspoon baking powder
- 1 teaspoon baking soda
- ¾ teaspoon salt
- 1 teaspoon ground cinnamon
- ½ teaspoon ground cloves
- ½ teaspoon ground allspice
- ⅓ cup oil
- ⅓ cup water
- 1 whole egg
- 1 cup applesauce
- ½ cup chopped nuts
- ⅔ cup raisins

Sift together first eight ingredients and place in large mixing bowl. Combine oil, water, and egg; add to dry ingredients; mix by beating 25 vigorous strokes by hand. Stir in applesauce, then nuts and raisins. Turn into a lightly oiled 13 x 9-inch pan. Bake at 350°F. for 25-35 minutes or until toothpick inserted in center comes out clean.

Yield: 20 servings
1 serving = ¾ teaspoon oil

Madcap Applesauce Cake

- 1½ cups flour
- 1 cup sugar
- 3 tablespoons cocoa
- ½ teaspoon salt
- 1 teaspoon baking soda
- ¼ cup plus 1 tablespoon oil
- 1 teaspoon vanilla
- 1 cup applesauce

Grease an 8-inch square pan. Combine all dry ingredients in pan. Make wells in corners of pan for liquid ingredients. Mix oil, vanilla, and applesauce; pour mixture into the dry wells. Mix thoroughly in pan and bake for 35-40 minutes at 350°F.

Yield: 16 servings
1 serving = 1 teaspoon oil

Devil's Food Cake

- 2 cups sifted cake flour
- ½ cup cocoa
- 1¼ teaspoons baking soda
- 1 teaspoon salt
- ½ cup oil
- 1¾ cups packed brown sugar
- 1 whole egg
- 1 cup skim milk
- 2 tablespoons vinegar
- 1 teaspoon vanilla

Sift together flour, cocoa, soda, and salt three times. Combine oil and sugar and beat until creamy. To sugar mixture, add the egg and beat well. Beat with an electric mixer at low speed, adding one-third of flour mixture, alternating with one-third of milk until all is used. Add the vinegar and vanilla and blend well. Pour into greased tube pan, lined in the bottom with lightly greased waxed paper. Bake at 350°F. for 35-40 minutes.

Yield: 15 servings
1 serving = 1½ teaspoons oil

Mississippi Mud Cake

- 2¼ cups sifted flour
- 2 cups sugar
- ½ teaspoon salt
- ½ cup oil
- 3 tablespoons cocoa
- 1 cup water
- 2 whole eggs
- ½ cup buttermilk
- 1 teaspoon baking soda
- 1 teaspoon vanilla

Sift together the flour, sugar, and salt. Bring oil, cocoa, and water to a boil, stirring, not beating. Combine the eggs, buttermilk, soda, and vanilla. Add the boiled mixture to the egg mixture; stir in the flour mixture. Pour into greased and floured 13 x 9-inch pan. Bake at 350°F. for 30 minutes.

Frost with Chocolate Glaze and sprinkle with 2 tablespoons chopped pecans.

Yield: 24 servings
1 serving = 1 teaspoon oil
1/12 egg

Chocolate Glaze

- ½ cup sugar
- 1½ tablespoons cornstarch
- 3 tablespoons cocoa
- dash salt
- ½ cup water
- ½ teaspoon vanilla

Combine sugar and cornstarch; add cocoa, salt, and ½ cup water. Cook and stir until thickened and bubbly. Remove from heat; add vanilla. While glaze is hot, frost cake. Covers a 13 x 9-inch cake.

Baked Devil's Float

- 1 cup sifted all-purpose flour
- ¼ teaspoon salt
- ½ cup sugar
- 2 teaspoons baking powder
- 1½ tablespoons cocoa
- ½ cup skim milk
- 1 teaspoon vanilla
- 2 tablespoons oil
- ½ cup chopped pecans

Topping:
- 1 cup packed brown sugar
- 5 tablespoons cocoa
- 1 cup boiling water
- powdered sugar

Sift together flour, salt, sugar, baking powder, and cocoa; place in medium-sized mixing bowl. In separate small bowl, combine milk, vanilla, oil, and pecans. Stir milk mixture into dry ingredients until batter is smooth. Turn into a lightly oiled 8-inch square pan. In another small bowl, combine brown sugar, cocoa, and boiling water; pour over top of batter. Bake in a 350°F. moderate oven for 30-40 minutes or until toothpick inserted in center comes out clean. Cool slightly and invert onto serving platter. Sprinkle top with powdered sugar.

Yield: 9 servings
1 serving = ⅔ teaspoon oil

Brownie Pudding

- 1 cup sifted all-purpose flour
- ¾ cup sugar
- 2 tablespoons cocoa
- 2 teaspoons baking powder
- ½ teaspoon salt
- ½ cup skim milk
- 2 tablespoons oil
- 1 teaspoon vanilla
- ¾ cup chopped pecans
- ¾ cup packed brown sugar
- ¼ cup cocoa
- 1¾ cups hot water

Sift together first five ingredients; add milk, oil, and vanilla; mix until smooth. Stir in nuts. Pour into a greased 8-inch square baking pan. Combine remaining ingredients; pour over batter. Bake at 350°F. about 45 minutes.

Yield: 9 servings
1 serving = ¾ teaspoon oil

Chocolate Miracle Cake

- 3 cups sifted flour
- 1½ cups sugar
- 2¼ teaspoons baking powder
- 1½ teaspoons baking soda
- ⅓ cup cocoa
- 1 cup mayonnaise-type salad dressing
- 1½ cups water
- 1½ teaspoons vanilla

Sift together the first five ingredients. Stir the salad dressing into the dry sifted ingredients. Gradually add to this the water and vanilla. Stir until smooth. Pour into two greased and floured 9-inch layer cake pans. Bake at 350°F. for 35-40 minutes or until cake tests done.

Yield: 12 servings
1 serving = 2 tablespoons oil

Israeli Matzo Cake

- 1 cup sugar
- 3 tablespoons cocoa
- ¼ cup red wine (sweet or semi-sweet, not dry)
- ½ cup margarine
- 6-7 whole matzos

Melt sugar, cocoa, and wine over low heat. Add margarine and stir until it melts. Then refrigerate mixture. Dampen (one at a time) 6-7 whole matzos in an even mixture of wine and water (let matzo absorb enough moisture to become pliable so that it won't break when handled, but not so soggy that it falls apart at the touch). Place one matzo in a shallow cookie sheet with sides. Spread cocoa mixture on matzo. Press a second matzo firmly on top of the first; spread more cocoa mixture on top, and repeat process until all matzo and chocolate are used up. Refrigerate and serve in slices.

Yield: 8 servings
1 serving = 3 teaspoons margarine

Date Cake

- ½ pound dates (approximately 1¼ cups)
- 1 teaspoon baking soda
- 1 tablespoon margarine
- 1 cup boiling water
- 1 whole egg
- 1 cup sugar
- 1½ cups sifted flour
- 1 teaspoon baking powder
- ½ teaspoon salt
- 1 cup drained crushed pineapple
- ½ cup chopped pecans
- 1 teaspoon vanilla

Heat oven to 350°F. Chop dates finely; add soda, margarine, and boiling water. Stir. Let stand until cool. Add egg, sugar, flour, baking powder, and salt. Stir thoroughly. Mix in pineapple, pecans, and vanilla. Pour into greased and floured 13 x 9-inch pan. Bake approximately 45 minutes.

Serve with Yogurt Sauce or Caramel Sauce (see recipes below).

Yield: 24 servings

Yogurt Sauce

- 1 cup low-fat yogurt
- ½ teaspoon vanilla
- ¼ cup sugar

Combine ingredients and blend. Top individual servings of Date Cake.

Caramel Sauce

- ½ cup sugar
- ½ cup brown sugar
- 2 tablespoons cornstarch
- ¼ teaspoon salt
- 1 cup boiling water
- 1 tablespoon margarine
- 1 teaspoon vanilla

Combine sugars, cornstarch, and salt. Add boiling water. Blend and cook over low heat until thickened. Add margarine and vanilla. Serve hot or cold poured over individual servings of Date Cake.

Spirited Holiday Cake

2¾ cups unsifted flour
3 teaspoons baking powder
½ teaspoon baking soda
½ teaspoon salt
¾ cup margarine
1½ cup sugar
2 teaspoons grated orange peel
3 eggs
½ cup skim milk
¼ cup orange juice
1 cup chopped pecans
    Rum Syrup
    Confectioners' Sugar Glaze
    red and green candied cherries

Combine flour, baking powder, baking soda, and salt; set aside.

Cream together margarine, sugar, and orange peel until fluffy. Gradually beat in eggs. Add flour mixture alternately with skim milk and orange juice, beginning and ending with dry ingredients. Mix in pecans. Beat until well blended. Turn batter into a well greased and floured 10-inch tube pan. Bake at 350°F. for 50 minutes until done. Before removing from pan, immediately prick surface with a fork or cake tester. Pour warm Rum Syrup over cake. After syrup is absorbed, remove from pan and place on wire rack to cool.

When cake is completely cooled, prepare Confectioners' Sugar Glaze. Pour and spread glaze over entire cake to form a smooth surface. Let dry for 10 minutes before decorating. Use red and green candied cherry pieces to make poinsettias and holly leaves.

Yield: 16 servings
1 serving = 2¼ teaspoons margarine
⅕ egg

Rum Syrup

In a saucepan combine ⅓ cup sugar and ¼ cup water; bring to a boil. Remove from heat and stir in ¼ cup orange juice and 2 tablespoons dark Jamaican rum.

Confectioners' Sugar Glaze

Combine 2 cups of confectioners' sugar, 3 tablespoons warm water, and ¼ teaspoon brandy extract in a bowl; beat until smooth. Glazes one 10-inch tube cake.

Cola Cake

¼ cup cocoa
1 cup cola
½ cup oil
2 cups sifted flour
2 cups sugar
1½ teaspoons baking soda
¾ cup buttermilk
2 whole eggs
1 teaspoon vanilla
½ cup miniature marshmallows

Mix together cocoa, cola, and oil in saucepan and heat to boiling point. Remove from heat and cool. Sift together flour, sugar, and baking soda. To these dry ingredients, add buttermilk, then eggs. Add cocoa mixture and vanilla, then mix with the electric mixer for 1 minute at medium speed. Pour into greased 13 x 9-inch cake pan. Sprinkle marshmallows over top of mixture and bake at 350°F. for approximately 35 minutes. Cool and frost with Cola Cake Icing.

Yield: 24 servings
1 serving = 1 teaspoon oil
½ egg

Cola Cake Icing

2 tablespoons margarine
2½ tablespoons cola
3 tablespoons cocoa
2 cups powdered sugar
½ teaspoon vanilla

Melt margarine and mix well with cola and cocoa. Add powdered sugar and vanilla; beat until smooth.

Yield: 24 servings
1 serving = ¼ teaspoon margarine

Pineapple Upside-Down Cake

Topping:
- 3 tablespoons margarine
- ¾ cup packed brown sugar
- 1 teaspoon grated lemon rind
- 1 tablespoon lemon juice
- 5 large canned pineapple rings, drained (reserve liquid)
- 5 red maraschino cherries

Cake:
- ¼ cup margarine
- ⅔ cup white sugar
- 1 whole egg
- 1 teaspoon vanilla
- 2¼ cups sifted flour
- 3 teaspoons baking powder
- ½ teaspoon salt
- ½ cup skim milk
- ½ cup liquid reserved from pineapple

In small mixing bowl, cream the margarine, brown sugar, lemon rind, and lemon juice. Spread evenly on bottom of lightly oiled 8-inch square pan. Arrange pineapple slices over mixture and place cherries in center of each slice.

In medium mixing bowl, cream ¼ cup margarine and ⅔ cup white sugar. Beat in egg. Stir flour, baking powder, and salt together. Add alternately with milk and pineapple liquid to the creamed mixture. Beat until smooth. Spread batter over fruit in baking pan. Bake at 350°F. for 45 minutes or until done. Remove from oven, let stand two or three minutes, and turn upside down onto a warm plate. Cool and serve.

Yield: 16 servings
    1 serving = 1⅓ teaspoons margarine

Prune Spice Cake

- 12 ounces pitted dried whole prunes
- 2 cups sifted flour
- 1½ cups sugar
- 1¼ teaspoons baking soda
- 1 teaspoon salt
- 1 teaspoon ground cinnamon
- 1 teaspoon ground nutmeg
- ½ teaspoon ground cloves
- ¼ cup oil
- 3 whole eggs
- 1 recipe Crumb Topping

Cover prunes with water. Simmer, covered, for 20 minutes. Drain, reserving ⅔ cup liquid, and cool. Chop prunes. In mixing bowl, combine flour, sugar, soda, salt, and spices. Add prune liquid and oil. Mix at low speed of electric mixer until blended. Beat at medium speed 2 minutes. Add eggs; beat at medium speed 1 minute longer. Stir in prunes. Pour into greased and floured 13 x 9-inch pan. Sprinkle with Crumb Topping. Bake at 350°F. for 35 minutes or until done.

Crumb Topping

- ½ cup sugar
- 2 tablespoons flour
- 2 tablespoons margarine
- ½ cup chopped pecans

Mix sugar and flour; cut in margarine until crumbly, and stir in nuts. Sprinkle evenly over the batter of the prune cake before baking.

Yield: 24 servings
    1 serving = ⅛ egg
        ½ teaspoon oil
        ¼ teaspoon margarine

Strawberry Shortcut Cake

- 1 cup miniature marshmallows
- 2 cups (2 10-ounce packages) frozen sliced strawberries in syrup, thawed
- 1 3-ounce package strawberry gelatin
- 2¼ cups sifted flour
- 1 cup sugar
- ⅓ cup margarine
- 3 teaspoons baking powder
- ½ teaspoon salt
- 1 cup skim milk
- 1 teaspoon vanilla
- 3 whole eggs

Generously grease the bottom only of a 13 x 9-inch pan. Sprinkle marshmallows over bottom of pan. Combine the strawberries and gelatin and set aside. Combine remaining ingredients, mixing at low speed with electric mixer until moistened. Beat 3 minutes at medium speed, scraping sides of bowl occasionally. Pour batter over marshmallows in pan. Spoon strawberry mixture evenly over batter. Bake at 350°F. for 45-50 minutes or until golden brown and a toothpick inserted in center comes out clean.

Variation: Use 1 quart fresh strawberries, hulled and sliced, instead of frozen berries. Use 1½ cups sugar in batter instead of 1 cup.

Yield: 20 servings
    1 serving = 1 teaspoon margarine
                       ⅐ egg

Zucchini Cake

- 3 cups grated zucchini
- 2 cups sugar
- ¾ cup oil
- 4 whole eggs
- ¾ cup chopped pecans
- 1½ teaspoons ground cinnamon
- 3 cups sifted all-purpose flour
- 2 teaspoons baking powder
- 1 teaspoon baking soda
- ½ teaspoon salt

By hand, mix together zucchini, sugar, oil, and eggs. Stir in nuts. Sift remaining ingredients together; stir into zucchini mixture. Pour into greased and floured 10-inch tube pan. Bake at 350°F. for 65-70 minutes. Let cake cool before turning out.

Yield: 25 servings
    1 serving = 1½ teaspoons oil
                       ⅙ egg

Carrot Cake

- 3 cups sifted flour
- 2 cups sugar
- 2 teaspoons ground cinnamon
- 1 teaspoon soda
- ½ teaspoon salt
- ¾ cup oil
- 1 teaspoon vanilla
- 3 whole eggs
- 3 cups grated carrots
- 1 8¼-ounce can crushed pineapple in syrup (do not drain)
- ½ cup chopped pecans (optional)

Sift dry ingredients together in a large bowl. Make a well in the center of this mixture and add oil and vanilla. Blend well until mixture resembles the consistency of pie dough. Beat in eggs. Add pineapple, carrots, and nuts (if desired). Bake in oiled and floured 13 x 9-inch pan for 45 minutes at 325°F.

Yield: 20 servings
    1 serving = ⅐ egg
                 2 teaspoons oil

Bourbon Balls

- 3 cups graham cracker crumbs
- 2 tablespoons cocoa
- 3 tablespoons bourbon whiskey
- ⅓ cup honey or light or dark corn syrup
- 1 cup ground pecans
    powdered sugar

Thoroughly mix ingredients together until a uniform consistency is obtained. Shape into balls approximately ¾ inch in diameter. Roll in powdered sugar. Store in airtight container.

Yield: 3 dozen balls

Brownies

- ¼ cup margarine
- 2 tablespoons oil
- 6 tablespoons cocoa
- 2 whole eggs
- 1 cup sugar
- 1 teaspoon vanilla
- ½ cup sifted flour
- ½ cup chopped pecans

Melt margarine in small saucepan. Remove from heat and stir in oil and cocoa until smooth. Cool. In medium-sized mixing bowl, mix eggs with sugar thoroughly by hand. To this, add vanilla, flour, pecans, and cocoa mixture. Mix well with spoon. Bake in a greased 8-inch square pan for 30-35 minutes at 350°F. Cool and cut into squares.

Yield: 16 servings
    1 serving = ⅛ egg
              1 teaspoon margarine

Peanut Brownies

- ⅓ cup oil
- ⅔ cup packed light brown sugar
- 1 whole egg
- ¾ cup sifted flour
- ¼ teaspoon salt
- 1 teaspoon baking powder
- ½ teaspoon vanilla
- ½ cup chopped peanuts

Blend oil and sugar together and stir in egg. Sift together flour, salt, and baking powder; combine with egg mixture. Add vanilla and peanuts. Spread in greased 8-inch square pan. Bake at 350°F. for 25-30 minutes. Cool and cut into squares.

Yield: 16 servings
    1 serving = 1 teaspoon oil

Cocoa Brownies

- ⅔ cup sifted all-purpose flour
- ¾ teaspoon baking powder
- ¼ teaspoon salt
- 2 egg whites
- ⅓ cup oil
- 1 cup sugar
- 6 tablespoons cocoa
- ½ cup chopped pecans
- 1 teaspoon vanilla

Sift together flour, baking powder, and salt. Slightly beat egg whites with fork; add oil to egg whites; mix. Blend sugar and cocoa into egg white mixture, adding each gradually. Stir in dry ingredients. Add nuts and vanilla; stir just until mixed. Turn into a lightly oiled 8-inch square pan. Bake in a preheated 350°F. oven for 18-25 minutes or until a toothpick inserted in center comes out clean. Do not overbake. Cool in pan. Frost if desired.

Yield: 16 servings
    1 serving = 1 teaspoon oil

Butterscotch Brownies

- 1 cup sifted all-purpose flour
- 1 teaspoon baking powder
- ½ teaspoon salt
- 1 cup packed light brown sugar
- 2 egg whites
- ¼ cup oil
- 1 teaspoon vanilla extract
- ¼ cup chopped pecans

Preheat oven to 350°F. Grease a 9-inch square pan. Sift all dry ingredients together. Whip egg whites lightly with a fork, then add oil and vanilla. Add dry ingredients to liquids and mix well. Fold in the pecans. Spread evenly in the prepared pan and bake in the preheated oven for 20 minutes. Cool and cut into squares.

Yield: 16 servings
    1 serving = ¾ teaspoon oil

Peanut Butter Bars

- 1 cup chunky peanut butter
- ¾ cup packed brown sugar
- 1 whole egg
- 2 tablespoons water
- 1 teaspoon vanilla
- ¾ cup sifted flour
- 1 teaspoon baking powder

Cream together peanut butter and brown sugar; blend in egg, water, and vanilla. Sift together flour and baking powder; stir into peanut butter mixture. Mix well. Spread mixture evenly in a lightly greased 8-inch square pan (batter will be stiff). Bake at 350°F. for 20-25 minutes.

Yield: 16 servings
      1 serving = 3 teaspoons peanut butter

Apricot Bars

- 1 cup all-purpose flour
- ¾ cup packed brown sugar
- 1 cup quick-cooking oats
- ¼ cup finely chopped nuts
- ¼ cup margarine (room temperature)
- 1 cup apricot jam
- powdered sugar

In mixing bowl, blend together the flour, sugar, oats, nuts, and margarine until mixture is crumbly. Press two-thirds of the mixture into a lightly oiled 8-inch square pan. Spread the apricot jam over this layer. Spoon the remaining crumbly mixture over the top to make the upper layer. Bake for 25 minutes at 350°F. Cool in pan. Sift powdered sugar lightly over the top. Cut into 16 bars.

Yield: 16 servings
      1 serving = ¾ teaspoon margarine

Cowboy Cookies

- 2 cups sifted flour
- 1 teaspoon baking soda
- ½ teaspoon salt
- ½ teaspoon baking powder
- ½ cup margarine
- 1 cup white sugar
- 1 cup packed brown sugar
- 2 whole eggs
- 1 teaspoon vanilla
- 2 cups quick-cooking rolled oats
- 1 cup raisins or chopped dates

Sift together flour, soda, salt, and baking powder. Thoroughly mix together margarine, white sugar, brown sugar, eggs, and vanilla. Add flour mixture to this gradually and mix well. Mix in rolled oats and raisins or dates. Drop by rounded teaspoonsful onto a greased cookie sheet. Bake 10-15 minutes at 350°F.

Yield: 5 dozen 2-inch diameter cookies
      1 cookie = ½ teaspoon margarine

Drop Sugar Cookies

- 2½ cups sifted flour
- ½ teaspoon baking soda
- ¾ teaspoon salt
- ½ cup margarine
- 1 cup sugar
- 1 teaspoon vanilla
- 1 whole egg
- 2 tablespoons milk

Have all ingredients at room temperature. Sift together flour, soda, and salt. Cream together margarine, sugar, and vanilla. Add egg; cream until mixture is fluffy. Stir in dry ingredients until mixture is smooth; blend in milk. Drop by teaspoonsful onto ungreased cookie sheet. Flatten cookies with bottom of glass lightly oiled and dipped in granulated sugar (try colored sugar for Christmas cookies). Bake at 400°F. for 10-12 minutes.

Yield: 3½ dozen cookies
      1 cookie = ½ teaspoon margarine

Zucchini Cookies

- 3 cups sifted flour
- 1 teaspoon baking powder
- 1½ teaspoons baking soda
- 1½ teaspoons salt
- 1 teaspoon ground cinnamon
- 1 teaspoon ground cloves
- ½ teaspoon ground nutmeg
- ½ cup margarine
- ½ cup white sugar
- 1 cup packed brown sugar
- 2 whole eggs
- 2 teaspoons vanilla
- 2 cups grated zucchini (peeled or unpeeled)
- ¾ cup raisins
- ½ cup chopped pecans

Sift together the first seven ingredients. In large bowl, cream margarine and sugars. By hand, beat in eggs and vanilla. Add dry ingredients alternately with the zucchini, mixing well after each addition. Stir in raisins and nuts.

Drop by teaspoons on greased cookie sheet. Bake at 350°F. about 10 minutes until edges begin to turn brown. Leave cookies on baking sheet for a minute before removing them to a rack to cool.

Yield: 6½ dozen cookies
1 cookie = ⅓ teaspoon margarine

Soft Molasses Cookies

- ⅓ cup margarine
- ¼ cup packed brown sugar
- 1 whole egg
- ¾ cup molasses
- 1 teaspoon ground ginger
- ¾ teaspoon ground allspice
- ¾ teaspoon ground cinnamon
- ¼ cup boiling water
- 2½ cups sifted flour
- 2 teaspoons baking soda
- ¼ teaspoon salt
  strawberry or currant jelly

Cream together margarine and brown sugar. Add molasses and egg, beating well. Sift together ginger, cinnamon, allspice, and 1 cup of flour; add to the creamed mixture. Add boiling water and blend. Add ½ cup flour and stir until blended. Chill dough for 30 minutes.

Combine 1 cup of flour, soda, and salt; sift three times. Add flour mixture to chilled dough and chill for at least another hour. Roll dough into 1-inch balls and make thumb print in each. Put dab of jelly in thumb print. Bake at 350°F. for 10 minutes on greased cookie sheet.

Yield: 4 dozen 2½-inch diameter cookies
1 cookie = ⅓ teaspoon margarine

Christmas Gingersnaps

(Julpepparkakor — Sweden)

- ⅓ cup water
- ⅓ cup dark corn syrup
- ¾ cup packed light brown sugar
- ½ cup margarine
- 1½ teaspoons ground cinnamon
- 1½ teaspoons ground ginger
- 1 teaspoon ground cloves
- 1½ teaspoons baking soda
- 4 cups sifted flour

Bring water, corn syrup, and sugar to a boil. Add margarine and stir occasionally until margarine is melted. Chill. Add spices and baking soda mixed with a small amount of flour. Gradually stir in remaining flour until the dough is soft. Turn dough onto a board and work until smooth. (Dough may be refrigerated for a few hours if it is too soft to work.)

Using pastry cloth, roll dough thin (about ⅛ inch), and cut out cookies with round or fancy cutter. Place on greased cookie sheet and bake in 450°F. oven 8-10 minutes. Let cool before transferring to rack.

Decorate, if desired, with icing. To make icing, combine 1¾-2 cups powdered sugar and 1 egg white and beat until smooth. Force icing through fine paper tube.

Yield: 6 dozen 2-inch cookies
6 cookies = 1 teaspoon margarine

Christmas Fruitcake Drops

- 1 cup sugar
- ½ cup margarine
- 1 whole egg
- 1 cup sifted all-purpose flour
- ¼ teaspoon salt
- ½ teaspoon ground cinnamon
- ¼ teaspoon baking soda
- ½ cup chopped pecans
- 2 tablespoons brandy (or ¾ teaspoon rum or vanilla extract)
- ½ cup candied red cherries
- ½ cup chopped candied pineapple
- 1¾ cups dates, chopped
- ½ cup blanched almonds

Preheat oven to 350°F. Cream margarine and sugar until light and fluffy. Add egg slowly and cream until well mixed. Combine flour and other dry ingredients; mix well. Add brandy (rum flavoring or vanilla). Add fruit, nuts, and dates. Mix in, but do not mash fruit. Drop cookies onto greased cookie sheet by the teaspoon. Bake at 350°F. for 12-15 minutes until light brown.

Yield: 4 dozen cookies
1 cookie = ¼ teaspoon margarine

Sand Tarts

- ¾ cup margarine
- 2 tablespoons sugar
- 2 cups sifted flour
- ¼ teaspoon almond flavoring
- ½ teaspoon vanilla
- ½ cup finely chopped pecans
  powdered sugar

Preheat oven to 400°F. Cream margarine and sugar. Add flour, almond flavoring, and vanilla; mix well. Add chopped pecans and mix. Form dough into small balls, about ¾-1 inch in diameter. Bake for 10-12 minutes on greased cookie sheet. Cool and then roll in powdered sugar. Store in airtight container.

Yield: 5 dozen
1 cookie = ½ teaspoon margarine

Lace Cookies

- 6 tablespoons margarine (room temperature)
- 1½ cups packed dark brown sugar
- ½ cup sifted flour
- 2 ounces sliced almonds
- 2 teaspoons water

Preheat oven to 325°F. Cream together margarine and sugar. Add flour and nuts and mix well. Sprinkle one teaspoon of the water over mixture and mix well. Repeat with the other teaspoon of water. With fingers, press mixture into 1-inch diameter balls. Bake six at a time for 12 minutes on a greased cookie sheet, leaving as much space as possible between cookies and between cookies and sides of cookie sheet.

Allow cookies to cool on sheet until warm but not soft. Remove with thin spatula and place on wax paper until completely cool.

Yield: 3 dozen cookies
1 cookie = ½ teaspoon margarine

Pecan Pralines

- 1 cup sugar
- ½ cup packed light brown sugar
- ½ cup water
- 2 cups pecan halves
- 1 tablespoon margarine

In uncovered medium-sized saucepan, gently heat white and brown sugar with water until sugars are dissolved. Stir in pecans. Over moderate heat, stirring continuously, cook to 250°F. or until syrup forms a pliable ball when dropped into very cold water (soft ball stage on candy thermometer). Remove from heat; stir in margarine. Continue to stir until syrup is sticky and adheres to nuts. Working quickly, drop candy by heaping teaspoonsful onto a lightly oiled cookie sheet. Allow candies to cool before eating.

Yield: 12 large pralines
1 praline = ¼ teaspoon mar

Cranberry Candy

- 1 16-ounce can jellied cranberry sauce (not whole berry)
- 1 6-ounce package cherry or strawberry gelatin
- ½ cup sugar
- 1 envelope unflavored gelatin
- ½ cup chopped pecans (optional)
- 3 tablespoons sugar

Warm cranberry sauce in a covered, medium saucepan over low heat for 20-30 minutes or until sauce is nearly melted, stirring occasionally. Add flavored gelatin; continue to heat and stir until gelatin dissolves. Do not permit mixture to boil. Remove pan from heat and cool. When mixture begins to gel, mix in nuts if desired. Turn into a very lightly oiled 8-inch square pan. Refrigerate in pan 24 hours. Cut into cubes; roll in sugar.

Yield: 25 cubes

Flaky Pie Crust

- 1 cup plus 2 tablespoons sifted flour
- ½ teaspoon salt
- 1½ teaspoons baking powder
- 3 tablespoons oil
- 4 tablespoons water

Sift together flour, salt, and baking powder. With fork, blend oil with water in measuring cup until homogenized. Add to dry ingredients and mix lightly with a pastry blender or a fork. Form dough into a ball. Flatten dough slightly and roll out. (Some people find it easier to roll out this type of pie crust between two pieces of waxed paper.)

Yield: 1 9-inch pie crust; 8 servings
  1 serving = 1 teaspoon oil

Cheesecake

Crust:
- 1 cup graham cracker crumbs (about 18 squares)
- ¼ cup margarine (room temperature)

Filling:
- 6 ounces Neufchatel cheese
- 1½ cups low-fat (2%) cottage cheese
- 1 whole egg
- ½ cup sugar
- ¼ teaspoon ground nutmeg
- 1 teaspoon vanilla

Combine graham cracker crumbs and margarine in a bowl. Mix well with a pastry blender, fingers, or a fork. Press mixture into a 9-inch pie pan. In blender, blend neufchatel and cottage cheeses together until completely smooth. Add egg, sugar, nutmeg, and vanilla; blend well. Pour the mixture into graham cracker crust and bake at 350°F. for 30 minutes, then turn oven off and allow to remain in oven 5 minutes longer. Chill.

Yield: 8 servings
  1 serving = ¾ dairy equivalent
              1½ teaspoons margarine
              ⅛ egg

Whipped Topping

- 1 envelope unflavored gelatin
- 4 teaspoons water
- ⅓ cup boiling water
- 1 cup ice water
- 1⅓ cups instant nonfat dry milk powder
- 6 tablespoons sugar
- 2 tablespoons oil
- 1 teaspoon vanilla
- 2 teaspoons lemon juice

Chill a large, electric mixer bowl and the beaters. In a cup, sprinkle gelatin over 4 teaspoons water and allow to stand 3 minutes. Add boiling water and stir until completely dissolved. Cool to room temperature. Soften over hot water if it begins to set. In the chilled bowl, combine ice water and powdered milk. Beat at high speed until soft peaks form (about 5 minutes). (If mixture spatters, drape tea towel or waxed paper loosely over bowl and beaters.) Gradually add sugar. Scrape sides of bowl and continue to beat. Gradually add oil, vanilla, lemon, and gelatin mixture. Scrape bowl sides and beat 1 minute more. Refrigerate.

Yield: 5-6 cups
  1 cup = 1 teaspoon oil

Lemon Lite Pie

Filling:
- 2 tablespoons lemon juice
- 2 tablespoons water
- 1 envelope unflavored gelatin
- ⅓ cup sugar
- ½ cup skim milk
- 1 teaspoon vanilla
- 2 cups low-fat (2%) cottage
- 1 whole egg

Put lemon juice, water, and gelatin in blender and blend for 30 seconds. Add sugar. Bring milk to boiling point; add to mixture in blender and blend 2-3 seconds. Add vanilla and blend 30 seconds at medium speed. Add cottage cheese and blend on high speed until creamy, about 30-45 seconds. Add egg and blend another 15 seconds until well blended. Pour into graham cracker crust and refrigerate 2 hours. Top with canned cherry or blueberry pie filling if desired.

Crust:
- 1¼ cup crushed graham crackers (20 squares)
- ¼ cup margarine (room temperature)

Mix ingredients together with fork until margarine is well distributed. Press into 9-inch pie plate.

Yield: 8 servings
1 serving = 1½ teaspoons margarine

Tangy Chocolate Pie

Substitute 2 tablespoons water for lemon juice. Add 2 tablespoons cocoa and ⅓ cup extra sugar where sugar is called for in filling recipe above. Proceed as for Lemon Lite Pie.

Pumpkin Lite Pie

Substitute 2 tablespoons water for lemon juice. Replace 1 cup cottage cheese with 1 cup canned pumpkin. Add ½ teaspoon ground cinnamon and ¼ teaspoon nutmeg to blender. Proceed as for Lemon Lite Pie.

Chocolate Mousse-Meringue Pie

Meringue:
- 4 egg whites, at room temperature
- ⅛ teaspoon salt
- 1⅓ cups sugar
- 1 teaspoon white distilled vinegar

Filling:
- 4 egg yolks
- ⅓ cup fresh orange juice
- 1 teaspoon grated fresh orange rind
- ½ cup sugar
- ½ cup cocoa, sifted
- 1 teaspoon instant espresso coffee
- 4 egg whites, at room temperature
- ½ cup sugar

Meringue: Beat egg whites with electric mixer until soft peaks form. Add salt. Gradually add sugar, beating until stiff and glossy peaks form and all sugar is dissolved. Speed of electric mixer will need to be gradually increased. Add vinegar and beat until well blended. Turn into a lightly oiled 9 x 3-inch springform pan, spreading meringue with spatula in even layer across bottom and half way up side. Bake at 275°F. about 60 minutes until firm and very lightly browned. Cool slightly on wire rack before adding filling.

Filling: Combine all ingredients except 4 egg whites and ½ cup sugar in top of double boiler. Cook and stir over boiling water until mixture is very thick. Cool. With electric mixer, beat egg whites in large bowl to soft peak stage. Gradually add sugar, beating until stiff, but not dry, peaks form. With spatula, fold chocolate mixture* into beaten egg whites very gently and with as few motions as possible. Pour into baked meringue shell and bake at 400°F. 10 minutes. Release and remove side of pan immediately after baking. Cool on wire rack. May be served hot or cold. Refrigerate if not served immediately.

*May need to add small amount of beaten egg whites to chocolate before folding into remaining beaten egg whites.

Yield: 12 servings
1 serving = ⅓ egg

Index

Acorn Squash, Stuffed 52
Almond
   Sauce with Salmon Loaf 47
   Candied 19
   Chicken 37
   Chicken Pâté 12
Anchovy Tuna Appetizers 14
Antipasto, Vegetable 14
Appetizers **9-19**
   Bourbon Balls 77
   Green Pepper 14
   Italian Nuts and Bolts 19
   Miniature Puffs 19
   Tuna Anchovy 14
   Tuna Balls 16
   Wakefield Specials 16
Apple
   Cake, Fresh 71
   Cake, Passover 72
   Cake, Roman 71
   Coffee Cake 64
Applesauce
   Cake 72
   Cake, Madcap 72
Apricot
   Bars 79
   Orange Bread 61
Asparagus, Oriental 51
Avocado
   Dip 10
   Guacamole Dip 11
Bagels, Matzo 65
Baking Mix 18
   Deviled Ham Puffs 18
Banana Nut Bread 61
Barbecued
   Chicken Orientale 38
   Pot Roast 29
   Sweet and Sour Baked Chicken 36
Bars
   Apricot 79
   Peanut Butter 79
Bean
   Black 54
   Dip 11
   Green Beans Lyonnaise 54
Beef 26-33
   Barbecued Pot Roast 29
   Bavarian Dinner 30
   Curried Kabobs 33
   Marinated Teriyaki 17
   Mushroom 28
   Parmigiana 27
   Pepper Steak 27
   Piquant 29
   Roast, in Beer 27
   Round Steak Casserole 28
   South-of-the-Border Strips 28
   Stew, Savory 28
   Stir-Fried and Vegetables 26

Beef, Ground
   Hamburger Stew 30
   Lemon Meatballs 32
   Porcupine Meat Balls 32
   Rice Party Casserole 31
   Souper Supper 30
   Summer Garden Stir-Fry 26
   Sweet-Sour Meatballs 16
   Tamale Pie 31
   Tasty Burger 32
Beer
   Beef Roast 27
   Bread 60
   Rabbit, Braised 34
Beets, Orange 54
Biscuits
   Easy 69
   Using Master Mix 68
Blueberry
   Coffee Cake 63
   Muffins 67
   Pecan Bread 61
Bouillabaisse, American Style 21
Bourbon Balls 77
Bran
   Six-Week Muffins 66
   Bread, Healthful 60
Breads **57-70**
   Apricot-Orange 61
   Banana Nut 61
   Beer 60
   Blueberry Pecan 61
   Bran, Healthful 60
   Brown 60
   Corn 67
   Cranberry 60
   Dilly 58
   Greek Easter 59
   Honey Pineapple 63
   Pecan Nut 62
   Pumpkin 62
   Rye, Jewish Sour 58
   Spoon, Easy 67
   Zucchini 62
Bread Stuffing 50
Breakfast Links
   Fruited Link Kabobs 15
   Snack Kabobs 15
Broccoli
   Fettucini, and 48
   Herb Seasoned 55
   Salad, and Cauliflower 23
Brownies 78
   Butterscotch 78
   Cocoa 78
   Peanut 78
   Pudding 73
Buns, Hot Cross 59
Buttermilk Coffee Cake 64
Cabbage, Crunchy Salad 23

Cake 71-77
   Apple, Fresh 71
   Apple, Passover 72
   Apple, Roman 71
   Applesauce 72
   Applesauce, Madcap 72
   Carrot 77
   Chocolate Miracle 74
   Cola 75
   Date 74
   Devil's Food 72
   Fruit 65
   Fruit, Fruitless 65
   Matzo, Israeli 74
   Mississippi Mud 73
   Pineapple Upside-Down 76
   Prune Spice 76
   Spirited Holiday 75
   Strawberry Shortcut 77
   Zucchini 77
California Dip, Mock 9
Can Size Table 7
Canapés, Chicken 13
Candy
   Almonds 19
   Bourbon Balls 77
   Cranberry 82
   Pecan Pralines 81
Caramel Sauce 74
Carrot
   Cake 77
   Marinated 23
   Super 55
Catfish, Curried 43
Cauliflower
   Salad, Broccoli and 23
   Savory 56
Cereal
   Italian Nuts and Bolts 19
   Granola Crunch 50
Cheese
   Ball 13
   Fondue 19
   Pastry Balls 18
Cheesecake 82
Cherry Coffee Cake, Montmorency 57
Chicken 35-41
   Almond 37
   Almond Pâté 12
   Barbecued Orientale 38
   Breast, on Rice 39
   Breasts in Curried Fruit 39
   Breasts, Stuffed Olé 39
   Canapés 13
   Cataloni 40
   Consommé, Cold 22
   Crunchy Coated 35
   Curry Sauce for 41
   French, in Sherry 38
   Fricassee 36
   Mushroom Cups 40
   Oriental Salad 40
   Poulet Dijon 37
   Poultry Olivini 41

   Smothered 35
   Spicy Baked 35
   Sweet and Sour Barbecued Baked 36
   Thigh Parmigiana 38
   Wings, Teriyaki 17
Chili Sauce Dip 10
Chips, Snappy Tortilla 12
Chocolate
   Cake, Miracle 74
   Glaze 73
   Pie, Mousse-Meringue 83
   Pie, Tangy 83
Chowder
   Manhattan Clam 20
   New England Clam 20
Clam
   Chowder, Manhattan 20
   Chowder, New England 20
   Linguini, with Clam Sauce 48
Coffee Cake
   Apple 64
   Blueberry 63
   Buttermilk 64
   Christmas 64
   Montmorency Cherry 57
   One-Step Tropical 63
   With Preserves 68
Cola Cake 75
   Icing 75
Confectioners' Sugar Glaze 75
Consommé, Cold Chicken 22
Cookies 69, 79-81
   Christmas
      Fruitcake Drops 81
      Gingersnaps 80
   Cowboy 79
   Drop (using Master Mix) 69
      Orange Flavored 69
      Spice 69
   Lace 81
   Molasses, Soft 80
   Sugar, Drop 79
   Zucchini 80
Cooking Tips 6-8
Cooking Terms 7-8
Corn Bread 67
Corn Casserole 53
Cornmeal Dumplings 36
Cornish Game Hen, Glazed 41
Cottage Cheese, Quick Dip 10
Cranberry
   Candy 82
   Nut Loaf 60
Crab Cakes 46
Curry
   Catfish 43
   Chicken Breast, in Fruit 39
   Dip 10
   Dip, variation 11
   Kabobs 33
   Sauce for Chicken 41
   Spinach Salad 24

Date
  Cake 74
  Muffins, and Orange 66
Definitions **4**
Desserts **71-83**
Dilly Bread 58
Dips 9-11
  Avocado 10
  Bean 11
  Chili Sauce 10
  Curry 10
  Curry, variation 11
  Green Goddess 9
  Guacamole 11
  Mock California 9
  Mock Sour Cream 9
  Peppery Olive 9
  Quick Cottage 10
  Rainbow Relish 11
  Seven-Layer Vegetable 10
  Spinach 9
  Tangy Vegetable 9
Dough, Fabulous Fluffy Roll 57
Doughnuts, Cake 70
Dressings, Salad 25
  Catalina 25
  Celery Seed 25
  Creamy Garlic 25
  Garlic French 25
  Sweet-Sour 25
Dressing, Rice 49
Dumplings, Cornmeal 36
Eggplant
  Parmesan 52
  Ratatouille 52
Fettucini and Broccoli 48
Fish **42-47**
  Creole 42
  Fillets in a Package 43
  Golden Puffs 45
  Greek, with Vegetables 44
  Herbed, Sauterne 44
  Mediterranean, Baked 43
  Molded Tuna Pâté 12
  Oven-Fried 44
  Sautéed, with Oranges 44
  Soups 20-21
  Steaks, Mexican 46
  Stew 21
  Tomato Crown 45
Flounder Marinara 45
Fondue 19
French Toast, Puffy 70
Fruit 71
  Cake 65
  Cake Drop Cookies 81
  Cake, Fruitless 65
  Chicken Breast, in Curried 39
  Link Kabobs 15
Gazpacho 21
Gazpacho Salad 25
Gingersnaps, Christmas 80
Grains **49-50**
Granola Crunch 50

Green Beans Lyonnaise 54
Green Goddess Dip 9
Green Pepper Appetizers 14
Guacamole Dip 11
Haddock, Highbrow 42
Ham
  Deviled Puffs 18
  Exquisite Marinated 33
  Pineapple Tidbits 15
  Quick-Stir, and Spinach 34
Honey Pineapple Bread 63
Icing, Cola Cake 75
Ingredient substitutions 6
Kabobs
  Curried 33
  Fruited Link 15
  Snack 15
Lemon
  Meatballs 32
  Pie, Lite 83
Lobster Bisque 20
Marinated
  Carrots 23
  Ham, Exquisite 33
  Mushrooms 15
  Pork Chops 34
  Teriyaki Beef 17
  Teriyaki Chicken Wings 17
Master Mix 68
Matzo
  Bagels 65
  Balls 22
  Cake 74
Meat **26-34**
Meatballs
  Lemon 32
  Porcupine 32
  Sweet-Sour 16
Metric Conversion Factors 7
Microwave Oven Method 42
Mixes
  Baking 18
  Fabulous Fluffy Roll Dough 57
  Master 68
Mock Sour Cream 9
Molasses, Soft Cookies 80
Muffins
  Blueberry 67
  Date and Orange 66
  Using Master Mix 68
  Oatmeal 67
  Six-Week Bran 66
  Whole Wheat Pineapple 66
Mushroom
  Beef 28
  Chicken Cups 40
  Marinated 15
  Royale 17
  Salad, Fresh 23
  with Shallots 51
Nuts
  Almonds, Candied 19
  Banana Bread 61
  Cranberry Loaf 60

Italian Nuts and Bolts	19
Pecan Bread	62
Oatmeal Muffins	67
Okra with Tomatoes	55
Olive, Peppery Dip	9
Orange	
Beets	54
Bread, Apricot	61
Flavored Drop Cookies	69
Muffins, Date and	66
Rice with	49
Sautéed Fish with	44
Paella, Scallop	45
Pancakes	
Finnish Oven	70
Potato	53
Potato Latkes	53
Using Master Mix	69
Parsnips, Pineapple-Baked	54
Pasta	**48**
Fettucini and Broccoli	48
Linguini with Clam Sauce	48
Pastry	
Cheese Balls	18
Miniature Appetizer Puffs	19
Pâté	
Chicken Almond	12
Tuna, Molded	12
Peanut Brownies	78
Peanut Butter Bars	79
Pecan	
Bourbon Balls	77
Bread, Blueberry	61
Nut Bread	62
Pralines	81
Sweet Rolls, Maple	57
Peppers, Green	
Appetizers	14
Savory, Fried	51
Pepper Steak	27
Pie	
Chocolate Mousse-Meringue	83
Chocolate Tangy	83
Crust, Flaky	82
Lemon Lite	83
Pumpkin Lite	83
Pineapple	
Ham Tidbits	15
Baked Parsnips	54
Bread, Honey	63
Cake, Upside-Down	76
Muffins, Whole Wheat	66
Pizza	48
Pork	33-34
Chops, Marinated	34
Curried Kabobs	33
Sweet and Sour	33
Potato	
Latkes	53
Oven-Fried	53
Pancakes	53
Po-mato Bisque	22
Vichyssoise	22
Poultry	**35-41**

Pudding	
Baked Devil's Float	73
Brownie	73
Pumpkin	
Bread	62
Lite Pie	83
Rabbit, Beer-Braised	34
Rainbow Relish Dip	11
Ratatouille	52
Rice	
Beef, Party Casserole	31
Breast of Chicken on	39
Chinese Fried	49
Dressing	49
with Orange	49
Scallop Paella	45
Turmeric	50
Rye Bread, Jewish Sour	58
Rum Syrup	75
Salads	**23-25**
Broccoli and Cauliflower	23
Crunchy Cabbage	23
Crunchy Topping for	24
Gazpacho	24
Mushroom, Fresh	23
Oriental Chicken	40
Spinach, Curried	24
Vegetable, Molded	24
Salad Dressing	**23-25**
Salmon	
Loaf with Almondine Sauce	47
Soup	20
Salt, Watch Out for	**5**
Sand Tarts	81
Sauce	
Caramel	74
Yogurt	74
Scallop	
Paella	45
Tarragon-Sautéed	46
Seven-Layer Vegetable Dip	10
Soups	**20-22**
Souper Supper	30
Sour Cream, Mock	9
Spices, sodium content of	5
Spinach	
Chinese Style	56
Dip	9
Quick-Stir Ham	34
Salad, Curried	24
Spoon Bread, Easy	67
Squash, Stuffed Acorn	52
Stew	
Fish	21
Hamburger	30
Savory Beef	28
Strawberry Shortcut Cake	77
Stuffing, Bread	50
Substitutions for salt	5
Substitutions, ingredient	6
Sugar Cookies, Drop	79
Sweet Rolls, Maple Pecan	57

Sweet and Sour
  Barbecued Baked Chicken 36
  Dressing 25
  Meatballs 16
  Pork 33
Table of equivalents 6
Tamale Pie 31
Teriyaki
  Beef, Marinated 17
  Chicken Wings 17
Tomato
  Crown Fish 45
  Herbed Slices 24
  Okra with 55
  Po-mato Bisque 22
  Stuffed 55
Topping
  Crumb 76
  Crunchy, for Salad 24
  Whipped 82
Tortilla Chips, Snappy 12
Trout, Mountain 42

Tuna
  Anchovy Appetizers 14
  Appetizer Balls 16
  Imperial 47
  Molded Pâté 12
Vegetables 51-56
  Antipasto 14
  Dip, Seven-Layer 10
  Greek Fish and 44
  Salad, Molded 24
  Stir-Fried Beef and 26
  Summer Garden Stir-Fry 26
  Tangy Dip 9
Vichyssoise 22
Waffles 69
Wakefield Specials 16
Yogurt Sauce 74
Zucchini
  Bread 62
  Cake 77
  Cookies 80
  Ratatouille 52

Acknowledgments

These recipes were contributed by participants and their partners, staff, and friends of the Coronary Primary Prevention Trial.

Laura Iasiello-Vailas, Iowa Lipid Research Clinic (LRC) nutritionist, edited the recipes, supervised their testing and contributed to the editing of the manuscript. The recipes were tested at the Iowa Lipid Research Clinic's Nutrition Resource Center by Steven Wonder and Charlene Yates.

Colette Hoff, nutritionist at the Northwest LRC, coordinated the collection of the recipes and edited the manuscript. Recipes were gathered by the following committee of LRC nutritionists:

Susan Grimes, Washington University, St. Louis, Missouri
Virginia Hartmuller, Johns Hopkins Medical Center, Baltimore, Maryland
Edith Hogan, George Washington University, Washington, D.C.
Colette Hoff, chairperson, Northwest Lipid Research, Seattle, Washington
Margot Maarleveld, Stanford University, Palo Alto, California
Mary McMann, Oklahoma Medical Research Foundation, Oklahoma City, Oklahoma
Katherine Moore, Oklahoma Medical Research Foundation, Oklahoma City, Oklahoma
Karen Smith, The University of Iowa, Iowa City, Iowa

Virginia Keating, program office nutritionist at the National Institute of Health, Washington, D.C., and Linda Snetselaar, director of the Nutrition Resource Center, The University of Iowa, are to be commended for their effective coordination of this project.

Special thanks are extended to Beth Burrows, Barbara Retzlaff, Judi Standley, and Dorothy Hollenbeck, nutritionists at the Seattle LRC, for their assistance in proofreading, as well as for their moral support.

Appreciation also goes to Dorothy Reedy and Marjorie Ross of the Seattle LRC and Jody Hyde of the Iowa LRC for their assistance in typing the manuscript, and to the Iowa LRC staff members for evaluations of the recipes.